Que®

MW00743454

Quicken® 5
Quick Reference

Linda A. Flanders

Quicken® 5 Quick Reference.

Library of Congress Catalog Number: 91-67623

ISBN: 0-88022-900-4

94 93 92   4 3 2

Interpretation of the printing code: the rightmost double-digit number is the year of the book's printing; the rightmost single-digit number is the number of the book's printing. For example, a printing code of 92-4 shows that the fourth printing of the book occurred in 1992.

This book is based on Quicken Version 5.0.

Que Quick Reference Series

The *Que Quick Reference Series* is a portable resource of essential microcomputer knowledge. Drawing on the experience of many of Que's best-selling authors, this series helps you easily access important program information. The *Que Quick Reference Series* includes these titles:

1-2-3 for DOS Release 2.3 Quick Reference
1-2-3 for DOS Release 3.1+ Quick Reference
1-2-3 for Windows Quick Reference
1-2-3 Release 2.2 Quick Reference
Allways Quick Reference
AutoCAD Quick Reference, 2nd Edition
Batch Files and Macros Quick Reference
CheckFree Quick Reference
CorelDRAW! Quick Reference
dBASE IV Quick Reference
Excel for Windows Quick Reference
Fastback Quick Reference
Hard Disk Quick Reference
Harvard Graphics Quick Reference
LapLink Quick Reference
Microsoft Word 5 Quick Reference
Microsoft Word Quick Reference
Microsoft Works Quick Reference
MS-DOS 5 Quick Reference
MS-DOS Quick Reference
Norton Utilities Quick Reference
PageMaker 4 for the Mac Quick Reference
Paradox 3.5 Quick Reference
PC Tools 7 Quick Reference
Q&A 4 Quick Reference
QuarkXPress 3.1 Quick Reference
Quattro Pro Quick Reference
Quicken 5 Quick Reference
System 7 Quick Reference
UNIX Programmer's Quick Reference
UNIX Shell Commands Quick Reference
Windows 3 Quick Reference
WordPerfect 5.1 Quick Reference
WordPerfect for Windows Quick Reference
WordPerfect Quick Reference

Publisher

Lloyd J. Short

Production Editor

Pamela D. Wampler

Technical Editor

Cory D. Garnaas

Production Team

Brad Chinn, Brook Farling, Sandy Grieshop, Denny Hager, Betty Kish, Bob LaRoche, Johnna VanHoose

Table of Contents

Introduction

Quicken 5 Quick Reference contains the quick reference information you need to manage your money with Quicken. This reference reviews the various commands, options, and functions available with Intuit's Quicken 5 Financial Management program for IBM compatible personal computers. You learn how to use Quicken and Billminder.

Quicken 5 Quick Reference highlights the most frequently used information and reference material that is required to work quickly and efficiently with Quicken.

Although *Quicken 5 Quick Reference* contains essential Quicken information, it is not intended as a replacement for the comprehensive information presented in a full-size guide. You should supplement this quick reference with Que's *Using Quicken 5*.

Now you can put essential information at your fingertips with *Quicken 5 Quick Reference*—and the entire Que Quick Reference Series!

HINTS FOR USING THIS BOOK

Keep the following conventions in mind as you use this book:

Keys you press or letters you enter appear in boldface, blue type. For example:

Press **Alt-R**-Reports from the Register.

On-screen information appears in digital type. For example:

Use the arrow keys to highlight <New Account>.

USING A MOUSE WITH QUICKEN 5

You can use any Microsoft-compatible mouse to select menu commands and options, display pull-down menus, move around the screen, display windows, or select items from lists. This section explains how to perform operations with a mouse in Quicken. The rest of the book, however, explains how to perform operations with the keyboard.

To select an option or command from a menu

1. Move the mouse on the table top so that the pointer highlights the option in the menu.

2. Press and release (click) the left mouse button.

To display a pull-down menu

1. Move the mouse on the table top so that the pointer highlights the menu title from within the menu bar at the top of the screen.

2. Click the left mouse button.

To select or highlight a transaction in the Register

1. Move the mouse on the table top so that the pointer highlights the transaction you want to select.

2. Click the left mouse button.

To open a window

1. Move the mouse on the table top so that the pointer highlights the label for the window in a selected transaction.

2. Click the left mouse button.

To choose an item from a list

1. Move the mouse on the table top so that the pointer highlights the item in the list.

2. Click the left mouse button twice in rapid succession (double-click).

To scroll up or down a Register or a list

1. Position the mouse pointer on a transaction from the Register or an item from the list.

2. Hold down the left mouse button and move the mouse up or down.

OR

1. Position the mouse pointer on the vertical scroll bar on the right side of the screen.

2. Hold down the left mouse button to begin scrolling.

To move to the next or previous transaction or list item

1. Position the mouse pointer on the up or down arrows on the vertical scroll bar on the right side of the screen.

2. Click the left mouse button.

To page up or down a Register or list

1. Position the mouse pointer on either side of the scroll box located on the right side of the screen. The position of the scroll box in the scroll bar represents your current position in the Register or list.

2. Click the left mouse button.

To record a transaction

1. Position the mouse pointer on the word Record at the bottom of the screen.

2. Click the left mouse button.

To escape

1. Position the mouse pointer on the word Esc at the bottom of the screen.

2. Click the left mouse button.

OR

   Click the right mouse button.

AN OVERVIEW OF QUICKEN 5

You can use Quicken to write and print checks, keep track of your bank accounts and investment portfolio, prepare a budget, create detailed reports, and obtain tax information.

Use Quicken commands for writing or printing checks, displaying financial reports, and entering transactions in the Register. You access Quicken commands through several different menus.

Starting Quicken

To start Quicken at the DOS prompt, change the current directory to the directory where you installed Quicken. If you used the default settings when installing the program, type CD\QUICKEN5. Press Enter. Then press Q and press Enter. DOS loads Quicken, and the Main menu appears.

Choosing menu items

Quicken 5 provides two menu styles: Alt-key and function-key. If you are installing Quicken 5 for the first time, the default menu style is the Alt-key menu. If you use Quicken 3 or Quicken 4 and are upgrading to Quicken 5, the default menu style is the function-key menu. Both menu styles are explained here; however, throughout this book, commands are explained using the Alt-key menu style.

To make a menu selection using the Alt-key menu style, press the highlighted letter within the menu choice. For example, press R from the Main menu to select the Use Register option.

To make a menu selection using the function-key menu style, press the number to the left of the menu choice. For example, press 1 from the Main menu to select the Use Register option.

Within the Register and the Write Checks screen, a menu bar lines the top row of the screen. The menu bar lists the titles of the pull-down menus available from the screen displayed. If you are using the Alt-key menu style, menu titles appear with a highlighted letter. Press the Alt key in combination with the highlighted letter to display the pull-down menu. For example, press Alt-E from the Register screen to display the Edit pull-down menu. If you are using the function-key menu style, a function key appears with each menu title. Press a function key to pull down the corresponding menu. For example, press F3 from the Register screen to display the Edit pull-down menu.

After a pull-down menu is displayed, you can use the left- and right-arrow keys ($\leftarrow$ and $\rightarrow$) to rotate through all the other pull-down menus.

Writing checks

Use the Write Checks screen to enter checks you want to print with Quicken. Enter all other transactions in the Register. Display the Write Checks screen from the Main menu by pressing W-Write/Print Checks. The Write Checks screen appears with a copy of a paper check on the screen. The program automatically makes an entry in the Register for every check you create within this screen. Use the available editing keys to move around the screen and enter a new check. You also can delete or edit a previously written check from this screen.

Recording transactions

The Register is Quicken's electronic record of your accounts. Use the Register to record all transactions that affect your account balance. Access the Register by pressing R-Use Register from the Main menu. You can switch to the Register from the Write Checks screen by pressing Ctrl-R. You can enter a transaction into the account or delete and edit previously entered transactions from the Register.

Canceling commands

You can abort almost any command in Quicken by pressing Esc. After pressing Esc, you go back a level in the menu structure or return to the Main menu. If you are at the Main menu, you can exit the program and return to DOS by pressing X-Exit.

Using alternate keystrokes

Initially, you may be confused because you often can accomplish the same task several different ways.

Suppose, for example, that you want to see the list of reports Quicken can create. You can accomplish the task in several ways:

Press C-Create Reports from the Main menu.

OR

Press Alt-R-Reports from the Register.

OR

Press Alt-R-Reports from the Write Checks screen.

As you gain more experience with Quicken, you will learn different keystroke combinations that enable you to work faster within the program.

Using keyboard speed keys

Following is a list of keyboard speed keys available from noninvestment Registers, the Write Checks screen, and Report screens:

Key(s)	*Action*
Ctrl-A	Select or set up account
Ctrl-B	Find previous (Backward) transaction
Ctrl-C	Select or set up category
Ctrl-D	Delete transaction/item
Ctrl-E	Edit account, category, class, or Quicken file

Key(s)	Action
Ctrl-F	Display Find Transaction window
Ctrl-G	Go to specific date
Ctrl-Ins	Insert transaction
Ctrl-J	Select transaction group
Ctrl-L	Select or set up class
Ctrl-M	Memorize transaction/report
Ctrl-N	Find next transaction
Ctrl-O	Display on-screen calculator
Ctrl-P	Print
Ctrl-R	Go to register
Ctrl-S	Create a split transaction
Ctrl-T	Recall memorized transaction
Ctrl-Enter	Record transaction
Ctrl-V	Void transactions
Ctrl-W	Go to Write Checks screen
Ctrl-X	Go to Transfer account
Ctrl-Z	QuickZoom

Following is a list of keyboard speed keys available from the investment account Register:

Key(s)	Action
Ctrl-L	List actions
Ctrl-Y	List securities
Ctrl-U	Update prices
Ctrl-B	Use previous day's date for recording market prices
Ctrl-N	Use next day's date for recording market prices

Key(s)	Action
Ctrl-PgDn	Use one month later for recording market prices

Following is a list of keyboard speed keys available from the Main menu:

Key(s)	Action
Ctrl-B	Back up all files and remain in Quicken
Ctrl-E	Back up all files and exit Quicken

COMMAND REFERENCE

The following is an alphabetical listing of Quicken 5's features and functions. Many entries are the exact name of menu choices found in Quicken. Each entry includes a description of the menu choice, an explanation of the feature's purpose and use, and step-by-step instructions for using the feature.

A/P by Vendor Business Report

Purpose

Lists your business's current liabilities for goods and services and tells you how much money you owe.

To generate an Accounts Payable by Vendor report

1. Select C-Create Reports from the Main menu.

2. Select B-Business Reports.

3. Select P-A/P by Vendor.

4. Type a title and press Enter. (This step is optional.)

5. Preview the report by using the arrow keys to scroll the display.

6. Press Ctrl-P-Print when you are ready to print the report.

7. Enter the number of the printer you want to use if it is different from the default.

8. Press **Enter** or **F10** to print the report.

Note

See also *Customize Report* and *Filters*.

A/R by Customer Business Report

Purpose

Lists the amounts that your customers owe you.

To generate an Accounts Receivable by Customer report

1. Select **C**-Create Reports from the Main menu.

2. Select **B**-Business Reports.

3. Select **R**-A/R by Customer.

4. Enter a title and press **Enter**. (This step is optional.)

5. Press the **space bar** to toggle between including and excluding an account.

6. Preview the report by using the arrow keys to scroll the display.

7. Press **Ctrl-P**-Print when you are ready to print the report.

8. Enter the number of the printer you want to use if it is different from the default.

9. Press **Enter** or **F10** to print the report.

Note

See also *Customize Report* and *Filters*.

Account Balances Report

Purpose

Presents the balances from all your accounts on a given date and calculates your net worth.

To generate an Account Balances report

1. Select C-Create Reports from the Main menu.

2. Select A-Account Balances.

3. Enter a title and the date on which you want to base the balances. Press Enter.

4. Preview the report by using the arrow keys to scroll the display.

5. Press Ctrl-P-Print when you are ready to print the report.

6. Enter the number of the printer you want to use if it is different from the default.

7. Press Enter or F10 to print the report.

Note

See also *Customize Report* and *Filters*.

Accounts

Purpose

Stores your financial data within a Quicken file.

To select an account

1. Select A-Select Account from the Main menu, or press Ctrl-A from within Quicken.

2. Use the arrow keys to highlight the account you want to use. Press Enter.

   The Register for the account you selected appears.

To set up a new account

1. Select A-Select Account from the Main menu.

2. Use the arrow keys or press Home to highlight <New Account>. Press Enter.

3. Fill in the new account information in the Set Up New Account window.

4. Enter a number to indicate the type of account you want to create and press Enter.

Press 1 for a bank account.
Press 2 for a credit card account.
Press 3 for a cash account.
Press 4 for an other asset account.
Press 5 for an other liability account.
Press 6 for an investment account.

5. Type the name of the new account in the Name For This Account blank. Press **Enter**.

6. Type the balance for the account in the Balance blank and press **Enter**.

7. Type the starting date that the beginning balance (in step 6) relates to and press **Enter**.

8. Enter a description such as the account number or the financial institution from which the account is held. (This step is optional.)

9. Enter the credit card limit if you are creating a credit card account.

10. Press **Enter** to set up the account.

To edit the name and description of an account

1. Select **A**-Select Account from the Main menu.

2. Use the arrow keys to highlight the account you want to edit. Press **Ctrl-E**.

3. Type the new account name and description in the Edit Account Information window. Press **Enter**.

   Quicken does not permit you to change the account balance.

4. Enter the new credit card limit if you are editing a credit card account.

5. Press **Ctrl-Enter** to save the changes.

When you change the name of an account, any transactions linked to it are updated automatically to reflect the new name.

To delete an account

1. Select **A**-Select Account from the Main menu.

2. Use the arrow keys to highlight the account you want to delete. Press **Ctrl-D**.

3. Type **YES** to confirm that you want to delete the account.

4. Press **Enter** to complete the deletion.

Notes

Quicken stores all your financial data in one or more accounts. The program provides six different types of accounts. Each account is tailored to meet a specific purpose and to work with a certain kind of transaction. Each Quicken file has a limit of 255 accounts.

See also *Investment Accounts*.

Adjust Balance

Purpose

Revises the cash balance or share balance in an investment account to match the account statement.

Note

See *Investment Accounts*.

Archive Data

Purpose

Copies all transactions from prior years to an archive file.

Note

See *Year End File Activities*.

Backing Up Quicken Files

Purpose

Protects you from losing data.

To back up the current file to an unformatted disk

1. Select **R**-Use Register.

2. Select **Alt-A**-Activities.

3. Select **D**-Use DOS.

4. Type **FORMAT A:** or **FORMAT B:** at the DOS prompt, depending on the drive in which you inserted your blank disk.

5. Type **EXIT** to return to Quicken when the formatting process is complete. Label the disk "Quicken Backup" and insert it into the floppy drive.

6. Press **Alt-P**-Print/Acct to display the Print/Acct menu.

7. Select **B**-Back Up File.

8. Type the drive letter of the floppy drive to which you want to back up data. Press **Enter**.

   Quicken backs up the file. The system alerts you if there are any problems with the backup procedure.

To back up a specified file to a formatted disk

1. Select **P**-Set Preferences from the Main menu.

2. Select **F**-File Activities.

3. Select **B**-Back Up File.

4. Type the drive letter of the floppy disk to which you want to back up the data. Insert the disk into the drive. Press **Enter**.

5. Use the arrow keys to select from the window the file you want to back up. Press **Enter**.

   Quicken backs up the file. The system alerts you if there are any problems.

To back up the current file to a formatted disk

1. Select **R**-Use Register from the Main menu.

2. Select **Alt-P**-Print/Acct to access the Print/Acct pull-down menu.

3. Select **B**-Back Up File.

4. Type the drive letter of the floppy drive to which you want to back up data. Press **Enter**.

   Quicken backs up the file. The system alerts you if there are any problems.

To back up the current file to a formatted disk quickly

1. Press Ctrl-B from the Main menu.

2. Type the drive letter of the floppy disk to which you want to back up data. Insert the disk into the drive. Press Enter.

   Quicken backs up the file. The system alerts you if there are any problems backing up the file.

To back up the current file and exit Quicken

1. Press Ctrl-E from the Main menu.

2. Type the drive letter of the floppy drive to which you want to back up data. Make sure that the disk is in the drive.

3. Press Enter.

   Quicken backs up the file. If there are any problems backing up the file, the system alerts you.

Notes

Always make copies of valuable financial data. You should have a regular backup schedule you use to keep your data safe. Depending on how often you use Quicken, you should back up your Quicken data at least once a week. If you enter transactions every day, you may want to back up data daily. See *Backup Frequency*.

You may want to try the three-disk method of making backups. You keep three sets of disks, using a different one each time you back up your data. The first time you back up data, you use the first disk set. The second time, you use the second set. The third time, you use the third set. The fourth time, you reuse the first disk set. Using this method, you always have two sets of recent data should anything happen to one of your disk sets.

Backup Frequency

Purpose

Tells Quicken how often to remind you to back up the current file.

To set the backup frequency

1. Select **P**-Set Preferences from the Main menu.

2. Select **F**-File Activities.

3. Select **F**-Set Backup Frequency.

4. From the Backup Reminder Frequency window, select one of these options:

    1 to never be reminded to back up the current file

    2 to always be reminded to back up the current file

    3 to be reminded to back up the current file on a weekly basis

    4 to be reminded to back up the current file on a monthly basis

5. Press **Enter** to set the backup frequency.

Note

See also *Backing Up Quicken Files*.

Balance Sheet Business Report

Purpose

Combines the balances from all accounts to help you calculate your business's net worth on any particular day.

To generate a Balance Sheet report

1. Select **C**-Create Reports from the Main menu.

2. Select **B**-Business Reports.

3. Select **B**-Balance Sheet.

4. Type a title and the date through which you want the report to include transactions. Press **Enter**. (This step is optional.)

5. Preview the report by using the arrow keys to scroll the display.

6. Press **Ctrl-P**-Print when you are ready to print the report.

7. Enter the number of the printer you want to use if it is different from the default.

8. Press **Enter** to print the report.

Note

See also *Customize Report* and *Filters*.

Billminder

Purpose

Reminds you when you have checks to print and when transaction groups are due, and displays investment reminders.

To change the directory where Billminder looks for data files

Instruct Billminder to look for data files in a directory other than \QUICKEN5 by modifying your AUTOEXEC.BAT file. Then, after the program name, type the name of the directory where your Quicken files are saved. You could type, for example, the line BILLMINDER C:\INFO\MYDATA after the program name.

To make Billminder pause after displaying its message

Change the line in your AUTOEXEC.BAT file to end with a /P. For example, you could type the line BILLMINDER /P. When you turn on your computer, Quicken displays any messages and tells you to press **Enter** to continue.

To turn off Billminder

1. Select **P**-Set Preferences from the Main menu.

2. Select **R**-Automatic Reminder Settings from the Set Preferences menu.

3. Type **N** in the Billminder Active field in the Automatic Reminder Settings window.

4. Press **Enter**.

   Billminder is no longer active.

Budgeting

Purpose

Sets up budget amounts for the categories you use in Quicken.

To set up budget amounts for categories

1. Select W -Write/Print Checks or R -Use Register from the Main menu.

2. From the Write Checks screen or any noninvestment Register, press Alt -A -Activities.

3. Select B -Set Up Budgets to display the Budgeting screen.

4. Use the arrow keys to move through the monthly columns. Type a budget amount for some or all categories.

5. Press Ctrl -W to return to the Write Checks screen, or press Ctrl -R to return to the Register.

   Quicken automatically saves your budget amounts.

To set up budget amounts for subcategories and transfers

1. Select W -Write/Print Checks or R -Use Register from the Main menu.

2. From the Write Checks screen or any noninvestment Register, press Alt -A -Activities.

3. Select B -Set Up Budgets to display the Budgeting screen.

4. Press Alt -E -Edit.

5. Select S -Budget Subcats to display subcategories in the budgeting screen, or select T -Budget Transfer to display transfer accounts in the budgeting screen.

6. Use the arrow keys to move through the monthly columns. Type a budget amount for some or all subcategories and/or transfer accounts.

7. Press Ctrl -W to return to the Write Checks screen, or press Ctrl -R to return to the Register.

   Quicken automatically saves your budget amounts.

To set up budget amounts using actual data

1. Select **W**-Write/Print Checks, or **R**-Use Register from the Main menu.

2. From the Write Checks screen or any noninvestment Register, press **Alt-A**-Activities.

3. Select **B**-Set Up Budgets to display the Budgeting screen.

4. Press **Alt-E**-Edit.

5. Select **A**-AutoCreate to display the Automatically Create Budget window.

6. Type in the Copy From blank the time period from which you want actual data extracted. Press **Enter**.

7. Type in the Budgeting screen the number of the first month in which you want actual data recorded and press **Enter**.

8. Specify how actual amounts should be rounded. Press **1** to round to the nearest $1, **2** to round to the nearest $10, or **3** to round to the nearest $100. Press **Enter**.

9. Press **Y** for Quicken to compute and enter average amounts in the Budgeting screen.

10. Press **F10** to set up budget amounts.

To copy budget amounts to other months

1. Select **W**-Write/Print Checks or **R**-Use Register from the Main menu.

2. From the Write Checks screen or any noninvestment Register, press **Alt-A**-Activities.

3. Select **B**-Set Up Budgets to display the Budgeting screen.

4. Press **Alt-E**-Edit.

5. Select **F**-Fill Right to copy the highlighted budget amount to each month to the right in the current row, or select **C**-Fill Columns to copy the highlighted budget amount column to all months to the right in every row.

   Quicken automatically fills in each row or column.

6. Press **Ctrl-W** to return to the Write Checks screen, or press **Ctrl-R** to return to the Register.

   Quicken automatically saves your budget amounts.

To set up budget amounts that occur every two weeks

1. Select **W**-Write/Print Checks or **R**-Use Register from the Main menu.

2. From the Write Checks screen or any noninvestment Register, press **Alt-A**-Activities.

3. Select **B**-Set Up Budgets to display the Budgeting screen.

4. Use the arrow keys to highlight the category row you want to budget on two-week intervals.

5. Press **Alt-E**-Edit.

6. Select **W**-Two Week to display the Set Up 2 Week Budget window.

7. Type the amount you want to budget and press **Enter**.

8. Type the starting date for the two-week interval.

9. Press **F10** to set up two-week budget amounts.

To change the layout of the Budgeting screen

1. Select **W**-Write/Print Checks or **R**-Use Register from the Main menu.

2. From the Write Checks screen or any noninvestment Register, press **Alt-A**-Activities.

3. Select **B**-Set Up Budgets to display the Budgeting screen.

   Note that the Budgeting screen is displayed in 12 monthly columns.

4. Press **Alt-E**-Edit.

5. Select one of the following options:

   Q-Quarter to display budget amounts by quarter

   Y-Year to display budget amounts by year

To copy budget amounts from one Quicken file to another

1. Select P-Set Preferences from the Main menu.

2. Select F-File Activities.

3. Select S-Select/Set Up File.

4. Use the arrow keys to select the file with the budget amounts you want to copy to another file.

5. If necessary, press Alt-A-Select Account to select an account. Use ↑ and ↓ at the Select Account To Use screen to select an account and press Enter.

6. From the Register, press Alt-A-Activities.

7. Select B-Set Up Budgets to display the Budgeting screen.

8. Select Alt-F-File.

9. Select E-Export Budget to display the Save Budget to File window.

10. Type a name for the export file in the DOS File blank, and press Enter to create the file.

11. Press Esc to return to the Main menu.

12. Select P-Set Preferences from the Main menu.

13. Select F-File Activities.

14. Select S-Select/Set Up File.

15. Use the arrow keys to select the file to which you want to copy budget amounts.

16. If necessary, press Alt-A-Select Account to select an account. Use ↑ and ↓ at the Select Account To Use screen to select an account and press Enter.

17. From the Register, press Alt-A-Activities.

18. Select B-Set Up Budgets to display the Budgeting screen.

19. Select Alt-F-File.

20. Select I-Import Budget.

21. Type the name of the file you created in step 10.

22. Press **Enter** to copy the budget amounts.

The following is a list of keys you can use to move
quickly through the Budgeting screen:

Key(s)	*Action*
Ctrl-←	Moves left one screen
Ctrl-→	Moves right one screen
Tab	Moves forward one month
Shift-Tab	Moves back one month
'' or '	Copies the amount from the previous month to the current month
Home	Moves to the beginning of an entry field or to the first column in a row of calculated fields
Home-Home	Moves to the first column in a row of entry fields or to the upper left corner of the screen from a calculated field
Home-Home-Home	Moves to the upper left corner of the screen from an entry field
End	Moves to the end of an entry field or to the last column in a row of calculated fields
End-End	Moves to the last column in a row of entry fields or to the lower right corner of the screen from a calculated field
End-End-End	Moves to the lower right corner of the screen from an entry field

To print the Budgeting screen

1. Select **W**-Write/Print Checks or **R**-Use Register from
the Main menu.

2. From the Write Checks screen or any noninvestment Register, press **Alt-A**-Activities.

3. Select **B**-Set Up Budgets to display the Budgeting screen.

4. Press **Alt-F**-File.

5. Select **P**-Print Budgets, or press **Ctrl-P**.

6. Select the number of the printer you are using if it is different from the default.

7. Press **Enter** or **F10** to begin printing.

Notes

To use Quicken's budget capabilities, you must set up categories and assign transactions to categories.

You can generate budget reports that compare actual amounts with budgeted amounts and show the difference. Quicken provides two different budget reports: the Monthly Budget Personal Report and the Custom Budget Report.

See *Categories, Monthly Budget Personal Report, Custom Reports*.

Business Categories

Purpose

Identifies specific types of transactions that are used in your business.

Standard Business Categories in Quicken

The following chart lists the standard business categories that Quicken includes. The chart contains the tax category, its description, if it is a tax-related item, and its type.

Category	Description	Tax Rel	Type
Gr Sales	Gross Sales	*	Inc
Other Inc	Other Income	*	Inc
Rent Income	Rent Income	*	Inc

Category	Description	Tax Rel	Type
Ads	Advertising	*	Expns
Car	Car & Truck	*	Expns
Commission	Commissions	*	Expns
Int Paid	Interest Paid	*	Expns
L&P Fees	Legal & Pro Fees	*	Expns
Late Fees	Late Payment Fees	*	Expns
Office	Office Expenses	*	Expns
Rent Paid	Rent Paid	*	Expns
Repairs	Repairs	*	Expns
Returns	Returns & Allowances	*	Expns
Tax	Taxes	*	Expns
Travel	Travel Expenses	*	Expns
Wages	Wages & Job Credits	*	Expns

Notes

Business categories are basically your chart of accounts.

Assigning categories helps you indicate the purpose of a transaction. Quicken includes standard categories for both home and business.

You specify that you want to use Quicken's standard categories in the First Time Setup window when you install Quicken.

For information on creating, deleting, or printing categories, see *Categories*.

Business Reports

Purpose

Meets your common and customized business reporting needs.

To access the Business Reports menu

1. Select C-Create Reports from the Main menu.

2. Select B-Business Reports.

3. Select the report you want from the list of available business reports.

Available Business Reports

A/P by Vendor

Lists unprinted checks, grouped and subtotaled by payee. This report works on your bank accounts only.

A/R by Customer

Lists outstanding balances for each vendor categorized by month. Quicken preselects all your other asset accounts and enables you to verify the selection when generating this report.

Balance Sheet

Shows your net worth as a specified date. It uses the balances from all your accounts.

Cash Flow

Gives totals for the money you have received and the money you have spent for each category by month. This report works only on your bank, cash, and credit card accounts.

Job/Project Report

Totals your income and expenses for each class. This report uses all your accounts.

Missing Check

Lists transactions in check number order and identifies any missing check numbers. This report uses the current account.

Payroll Report

Totals your income and expenses for each payee, subtotaled by category. This report uses only those transactions that include the Payroll category. It uses information from all your accounts.

P & L Statement

Lists totals of your income and expenses for each category by month. This report uses all accounts. The profit and loss statement is a basic report required by all businesses.

Notes

Printing a customized business report (by setting report options) helps you determine exactly what information is reported. Setting a filter on your reports helps you define further which transactions your report includes.

For information on generating a business report, refer to the individual report name.

See also *Customize Report* and *Filters*.

Calculator

Purpose

Adds, subtracts, multiplies, and divides numbers.

To use the calculator

1. Press Alt-A-Activities from the Register or Write Checks screen.

2. Select C-Calculator, or press Ctrl-O.

3. Enter one number, press an arithmetic operation, and enter another number.

4. Press Enter.

To paste (copy) calculations into Quicken

1. Move the cursor over the blank where you will paste the calculation result.

2. Press Ctrl-O to access the calculator.

3. Complete the calculation.

4. Press F9-Paste to copy the answer from the calculator into your work.

Capital Gains Investment Report

Purpose

Shows long-term and short-term capital gains for securities sold during a specified time period.

To generate a Capital Gains Investment report

1. Select C-Create Reports from the Main menu.

2. Select I-Investment Reports.

3. Select C-Capital Gains Report.

4. Enter a report title. Press Enter. (This step is optional.)

5. Enter the transaction dates to be included in the report.

6. Enter a number corresponding to how you want the report subtotaled.

7. Enter a number between 1 and 365 for the number of days that are the maximum holding period permitted by current tax law.

8. Press C to include the current investment account in the report. To include all investment accounts, press A. To include selected investment accounts, press S. Quicken displays the Select Account To Use window for you to select the investment accounts to include in the report.

9. Press Enter and preview the report displayed on the screen by using the arrow keys to scroll the display.

10. Press Ctrl-P-Print when you are ready to print the report.

11. Enter the number of the printer you want to use if it is different from the default.

12. Press Enter or F10 to print the report.

Notes

Before using this report, you must tell Quicken the date you bought the shares you sold and the actual cost of these shares. Make sure that you enter this information in the Register for the investment(s) on which you want to report.

See also *Filters* and *Printing Reports*.

Cash Flow Business Report

Purpose

Totals your cash inflows and outflows for a specified period.

To generate a Cash Flow Business report

1. Select **C**-Create Reports from the Main menu.

2. Select **B**-Business Reports.

3. Select **C**-Cash Flow.

4. Enter a title. Press **Enter**. (This step is optional.)

5. Enter in the From and Through blanks the starting and ending dates for transactions. Press **Enter**.

6. Preview the report displayed on the screen; use the arrow keys to scroll the display.

7. Press **Ctrl-P**-Print when you are ready to print the report.

8. Enter the number of the printer you want to use if it is different from the default.

9. Press **Enter** or **F10** to print the report.

Note

See also *Customize Report* and *Filters*.

Cash Flow Personal Report

Purpose

Tracks the inflow and outflow of your money.

To generate a Cash Flow Personal report

1. Select **C**-Create Reports from the Main menu.

2. Select **P**-Personal Reports.

3. Select **C**-Cash Flow.

4. Enter an optional title and press **Enter**.

5. Enter in the From and Through blanks the dates between which you want to use transactions.

6. Preview the report displayed on the screen; use the arrow keys to scroll the display.

7. Press **Ctrl-P**-Print when you are ready to print the report.

8. Enter the number of the printer you want to use if it is different from the default.

9. Press **Enter** or **F10** to print the report.

Note

See also *Customize Report* and *Filters*.

Categories

Purpose

Specifies how your items of income and expense are distributed.

To create a new category

1. Select **W**-Write/Print Checks or **R**-Use Register from the Main menu.

2. Press **Alt-S**-Shortcuts.

3. Select **C**-Categorize/Transfer, or press **Ctrl-C**.

4. Press **Home** to highlight <New Category>. Press **Enter**.

5. Type the category name. Specify whether the category is for (**I**)income or (**E**)expense or if it is a (**S**)subcategory.

6. Type a description of the category. (This step is optional.)

7. Press Y if the category is tax-related. Press N if the category is not.

8. Press F9 if you want to assign a tax schedule to the category. Quicken displays the Tax Schedule window. Use ↑ and ↓ to highlight a tax schedule and press Enter. Quicken next displays the Tax Line window. Again, use ↑ and ↓ to select the tax line and press Enter.

9. Press Enter at the Set Up Category window to save the category information.

To assign a category to a transaction

1. Select W-Write/Print Checks or R-Use Register from the Main menu.

2. Enter transaction information in the Write Checks screen or the Register.

3. In the Category blank, type the category name, or press Ctrl-C to display the Category and Transfer List. Use the arrow keys to select a category from the list and press Enter.

4. Press Enter-Enter or F10 to record the transaction.

To demote a category to a subcategory

1. Select W-Write/Print Checks or R-Use Register from the Main menu.

2. Press Alt-S-Shortcuts.

3. Select C-Categorize/Transfer, or press Ctrl-C.

   The Category List appears, which lists both categories and subcategories.

4. Use the arrow keys to highlight the category you want to change to a subcategory.

5. Press F8.

6. Quicken moves the category name to the top of the Category and Transfer List.

7. Use the arrow keys to move the category to the category name for which the category will become a subcategory.

8. Press Enter. Quicken changes the category to a subcategory and, in the Category and Transfer List, positions the new subcategory name under the category name.

   Quicken makes changes to all previous transactions assigned to this category in the Register.

To merge a category with another category

1. Select W-Write/Print Checks or R-Use Register from the Main menu.

2. Press Alt-S-Shortcuts.

3. Select C-Categorize/Transfer, or press Ctrl-C.

   The Category List appears, which lists both categories and subcategories.

4. Use the arrow keys to highlight the category you want to merge with another category.

5. Press F8. Quicken moves the category to the top of the Category and Transfer List.

6. Use the arrow keys to move the category to the category line with which you want to merge.

7. Press Enter. Quicken makes the category you just moved a subcategory of the category with which you are merging.

8. Use the arrow keys to highlight the subcategory you just created, and press Ctrl-D to delete the subcategory.

9. Press Enter to confirm the deletion of the subcategory.

   Quicken makes changes to all previous transactions assigned to the merged category in the Register.

To delete a category

1. Select W-Write/Print Checks or R-Use Register from the Main menu.

2. Press **Alt-S**-Shortcuts.

3. Select **C**-Categorize/Transfer, or press **Ctrl-C**.

4. Use the arrow keys to highlight the category you
   want to delete.

5. Press **Ctrl-D**.

6. Press **Enter** to confirm the deletion of the category.

To edit a category

1. Select **W**-Write/Print Checks or **R**-Use Register from
   the Main menu.

2. Press **Alt-S**-Shortcuts.

3. Select **C**-Categorize/Transfer, or press **Ctrl-C**.

4. Use the arrow keys to highlight the category you
   want to edit.

5. Press **Ctrl-E**.

6. Enter a new category name at the Name field.

7. Press **I** if the category represents an item of income.
   Press **E** if the category represents an expense. Press **S**
   if the category represents a subcategory.

8. Enter or modify the description. (This step is
   optional.)

9. Press **Y** if the category is tax-related. Press **N** if the
   category is not.

10. Press **F9** if you want to assign or change the tax
    schedule. Quicken displays the Tax Schedule
    window. Use ↑ and ↓ to highlight a tax schedule and
    press **Enter**. Quicken next displays the Tax Line
    window. Again, use ↑ and ↓ to select the tax line and
    press **Enter**.

11. Press **Ctrl-Enter** from any blank in the Edit
    Category window.

To print the Category and Transfer List

1. Select **W**-Write/Print Checks or **R**-Use Register from
   the Main menu.

2. Press **Alt-S**-Shortcuts.

3. Select C-Categorize/Transfer, or press Ctrl-C.

4. Press Ctrl-P to print.

5. Enter the number of the printer you are using if it is different from the default.

6. Press Enter or F10 to begin printing.

Notes

You can name categories using words, numbers, or a combination of both. Category names can include up to 15 characters.

Quicken contains preset lists of home and business categories you can use to categorize basic personal and business income and expenses. See *Business Categories* and *Home Categories*.

You may want to assign a subcategory to a category. See *Subcategories*.

You can assign different amounts of the same transaction to different categories by splitting the transaction. See *Splitting Transactions*.

You now can assign categories to tax schedules. If you prepare your own income tax return, this report will assist in transferring amounts to the proper tax schedule of your return. See *Tax Schedule Report*.

CheckFree

Purpose

Uses your computer and a modem to pay bills electronically.

How Quicken works with the CheckFree service

1. You enter an Electronic Payment transaction into Quicken. Your transaction includes the scheduled date, which is when you want the payment made.

2. You use your modem. Quicken automatically dials the Checkfree Processing Center and transmits your payment instructions to the service.

3. The Checkfree Processing Center returns a confirmation number. Your Quicken Check Register is updated as soon as the electronic transmission is successfully completed.

4. The Checkfree Processing Center makes the payment for you in one of three ways: it electronically removes the money from your account and prints and mails a paper check; it mails a laser-printed check from the funds in your account; or it initiates an electronic payment directly from your bank account to the merchant.

5. You receive verification of the payment in your bank statement and in the statement you receive from the merchant.

To begin using CheckFree

1. Make sure that your computer has a Hayes compatible modem.

2. Call Intuit, the manufacturer of Quicken, to subscribe to the monthly service.

To set or change electronic payment settings

1. Select P-Set Preferences from the Main menu.

2. Select L-Electronic Payment Settings.

3. Select M-Modem Settings.

4. Type the number that corresponds to the port to which you attached your modem. Press Enter.

5. Type the modem speed that corresponds to the baud rate required by CheckFree. Press Enter.

6. Press T at the Tone or Pulse Dialing (T/P) blank if you have a push button phone. Press P if you have a rotary dial phone.

7. Enter in the next blank the telephone number you received from Checkfree Corporation. Press Enter.

8. Press Y at the Turn On Electronic Payment Capability (Y/N) blank.

To set up a bank account for electronic payments

1. Select P-Set Preferences from the Main menu.

2. Select L-Electronic Payment Settings.

3. Select A-Account Settings.

4. Use the arrow keys to highlight the bank account you want to set up. Press Enter.

5. Type Y in the Set Up For Electronic Payment blank. Press Enter.

6. Enter your name, address, phone number, and Social Security number in the Electronic Payment Account Settings window.

7. Enter the CheckFree Identification number you received from Checkfree Corporation.

8. Press Enter or F10 to set up the account for electronic payments.

To write an electronic check

1. Select W-Write/Print Checks from the Main menu. Make sure that the Write Checks screen displays a check in electronic payment format. To change the Write Checks screen to electronic payment format, press F9.

2. Type the information in the Write Checks screen.

3. Press Enter or F10 to record the electronic check.

To transmit an electronic payment

1. Select W-Write/Print Checks or R-Use Register from the Main menu.

2. Press Alt-P-Print/Acct.

3. Select T-Transmit Payments, or press Ctrl-I.

4. Press F9 to preview the transmission.

5. Use the arrow keys to scroll and review the payments in the Preview Transmissions to CheckFree window.

6. Press Enter to transmit the electronic payments.

Electronic payments that have not been transmitted contain greater than signs (>>>>) in the Num column of the Register; payments that have been transmitted contain E - PMT in the Num column.

Notes

CheckFree is a nationwide computer-based check payment service. Funds are deposited electronically through the Federal Reserve bank system.

If your check recipients are not set up to receive electronic payments, CheckFree prints and mails your recipients paper checks. Although the capability to use CheckFree comes with Quicken, you must subscribe to this additional service.

Before you can use CheckFree to pay your bills, you must turn on the electronic payment capability in Quicken.

═ Checks and Reports Settings ═

Purpose

Enables you to adjust checks and reports settings to fit your needs.

Explanations of other options

Extra message line on check (printed on check but not recorded)(Y/N). Press **Y** to print an additional line of text to the right of each check's address. You can use this additional line for comments.

Change date of checks to date when printed(Y/N). Press **Y** if you want all checks printed with the date.

Print months as Jan, Feb...on checks(Y/N). Press **Y** to print the date with the month spelled out in three-letter abbreviations.

Print categories on voucher checks(Y/N). Press **Y** if you want Quicken to print any category and description information on voucher checks. Press **N** if you don't want the category information printed, but you do want any description information printed.

Warn if a check number is reused(Y/N). Press **Y** to signal Quicken to warn you before recording a transaction if the check number you are using has been used previously.

In reports, print category Description/Name/Both (D/N/B). Press either **D**, **N**, or **B** to determine how categories and classes are labeled in reports. If you press D, Quicken prints the description when there is one and uses the category name if there is not.

In reports, print account Description/Name/Both (D/N/B). Press either **D**, **N**, or **B** to determine how accounts are labeled in reports. If you press D, Quicken prints the description when there is one and uses the account name if there is not.

To change the checks and reports settings

1. Select **P**-Set Preferences from the Main menu.

2. Select **C**-Checks and Reports Settings.

3. Use **Enter**, **Tab**, and **Shift-Tab** to move the cursor through the blanks. Change the settings for the option(s).

4. Press **Enter** or **F10** to save the checks and reports settings.

Classes

Purpose

Enables you to specify what information a transaction covers.

To create a new class

1. Press **Alt-S**-Shortcuts from the Register or the Write Checks screen.

2. Select **L**-Select/Set Up Class, or press **Ctrl-L**.

3. Press **Home** to highlight <New Class>.

4. Enter the name of the class in the Name blank.

5. Type a description of the class in the Description blank. (This step is optional.)

6. Press **Enter** or **F10** to create the new class.

To assign a class to a transaction

1. Select W-Write/Print Checks or R-Use Register from the Main menu.

2. Enter transaction information in the Write Checks screen or the Register.

3. In the Category blank, type the category name followed by a / and the class name. If you are not assigning a category to the transaction, just type a / followed by the class name.

   OR

   Press Ctrl-L to display the Class List. Use the arrow keys to select a class from the list and press Enter.

4. Press Enter-Enter or F10 to record the transaction.

To delete a class

1. Press Alt-S-Shortcuts from the Register or Write Checks screen.

2. Select L-Select/Set Up Class, or press Ctrl-L.

3. Use the arrow keys to highlight the class you want to delete.

4. Press Ctrl-D.

5. Press Enter to complete the deletion. To abort the deletion, press Esc.

To edit a class

1. Press Alt-S-Shortcuts from the Register or the Write Checks screen.

2. Select L-Select/Set Up Class, or press Ctrl-L.

3. Use the arrow keys to highlight the class you want to modify.

4. Press Ctrl-E to edit the class.

5. Enter a new name and description for the class. You can modify all or part of the current information.

6. Press Enter or F10 to complete the edit.

To print a list of the classes

1. Press Alt-S-Shortcuts from the Register or the Write Checks screen.

2. Select L-Select/Set Up Class, or press Ctrl-L.

3. To print the entire list of defined classes, press Ctrl-P.

4. Enter the number of the printer you want to use if it is different from the default.

5. Press Enter or F10 to print the Class List.

Collapse Reports

Purpose

Summarizes all detail for a row heading in reports.

To collapse a report

1. Select C-Create Reports from the Main menu.

2. Select the report you want to create from the next two menus.

3. With the report displayed on-screen, use the arrow keys to position the cursor on the row heading you want to summarize, or collapse.

4. Press Alt-L-Layout.

5. Select C-Collapse, or press –.

6. Quicken now displays one line for the row heading; however, the total for the row heading does not change.

Notes

The Collapse feature is available only for Summary, Budget, or Account Balances reports.

To return any report detail that has been collapsed to its original format, use the Expand option from the Layout pull-down menu. See *Expand Reports*.

Copy Quicken File

Purpose

Copies all or part of a file.

Note

See also *File Activities*.

Custom Reports

Purpose

Enables you to determine the information your reports include.

To see a list of the custom reports

Select C-Create Reports from the Main menu.

The Reports menu appears. The custom reports are listed in the bottom part of the Reports menu.

To create a custom report

1. Select C-Create Reports from the Main menu.

2. Select the type of report you want to create. You can select one of the following four reports:

   T-Transaction report
   S-Summary report
   U-Budget report
   A-Account Balances report

3. Type a report title in the first blank.

4. Enter the dates of transactions you want to include in the report in the Restrict To Transactions From and Through blanks.

5. Enter any other criteria specific to the type of report you are creating.

6. Press C to base your report on the current account. Press A to base it on all accounts. Press S to base it on select accounts.

7. If you chose to base your report on selected accounts, select the accounts you want to use. Use the arrow keys to highlight accounts. Press the space bar to toggle on or off the accounts.

8. Press F8-Options to set specific options. These report options enable you to:

   - organize the report
   - include/exclude transfers
   - include unrealized gains
   - show totals
   - show split transactions
   - show memos or categories
   - show cents
   - show subcategories and subclasses

9. Press F9-Filters to specify further which transactions to include in the report.

10. Press Enter at the Create Report window to view the report.

11. Preview the report displayed on your screen; use the arrow keys to scroll the display.

12. Press Ctrl-P-Print when you are ready to print the report.

13. Enter the number of the printer you want to use if it is different from the default.

14. Press Enter or F10 to print the report.

Notes

Transaction reports list individual transactions from the Register. Summary reports present totals based on categories, classes, payees, or accounts, without listing individual transactions. Budget reports compare actual income and expenses recorded in your accounts against budgeted amounts. Account Balance reports calculate the overall balance in accounts for a specified period of time.

See also *Filters* and *Printing*.

Customize Report

Purpose

Enables you to modify the format and content of Quicken's preset reports.

To generate a customized report

1. Select C-Create Reports from the Main menu.

2. Select P-Personal Reports or B-Business Reports.

3. Enter the type of report you want to generate.

   If you selected Personal Reports, you can select the following Personal reports:

   Cash Flow
   Monthly Budget
   Itemized Categories
   Tax Summary
   Net Worth
   Missing Check
   Tax Schedule

   If you selected Business Reports, you can select the following Business reports:

   P & L Statement
   Cash Flow
   A/P by Vendor
   A/R by Customer
   Job/Project
   Payroll
   Balance Sheet
   Missing Check

4. Enter an optional title and the dates you want the report to include.

5. Press F8 to set report options.

6. Fill in the Report Options window and press Enter.

7. Preview the report that is displayed on your screen; use the arrow keys to scroll the display.

8. Press Ctrl-P-Print when you are ready to print.

9. Enter the number of the printer you want to use if it is different from the default.

10. Press Enter or F10 to print the report.

Note

See also *Custom Reports* and *Filters*.

Date

Purpose

Confirms that your records are historically correct and that they match those of your financial institution.

To change how Quicken displays the date

1. Select P-Set Preferences from the Main menu.

2. Select T-Transactions Settings.

3. Use Enter to move the cursor to line 4. Select either M for month/day/year (MM/DD/YY) format or D for day/month/year (DD/MM/YY) format.

4. Press Enter to save the date format.

To change the date in the Register or Write Checks screen

1. Select R-Use Register or W-Write/Print Checks from the Main menu.

2. Highlight the Date field in the Register or the Write Checks screen.

3. Press:

+	to advance the date by one day
–	to move the date back by one day
T	to change the date to today's date
M	to change the date to the first of the current month
H	to change the date to the end of the current month
Y	to change the date to the first of the current year
R	to change the date to the end of the current year

Press any of the keys repeatedly to change the
date by more than one increment. For example,
press + four times to advance the date by four
days.

Deleting Information

Purpose

Deletes transactions in the Register or the Write Checks
screen, categories, classes, and account groups.

To delete transactions in the Register

1. Select R-Use Register from the Main menu.

2. Use the arrow keys to highlight the transaction you
   want to delete.

3. Press Alt-E-Edit.

4. Select D-Delete Transaction, or press Ctrl-D.

5. Select 1-Delete Transaction.

To delete transactions in the Write Checks screen

1. Select W-Write/Print Checks from the Main menu.

2. Use PgUp and PgDn to display the check you want
   to delete.

3. Press Alt-E-Edit.

4. Select D-Delete Transaction, or press Ctrl-D.

5. Select 1-Delete Transaction.

To delete categories

1. Press Alt-S-Shortcuts from the Register or Write
   Checks screen.

2. Select C-Categorize/Transfer, or press Ctrl-C.

3. Use the arrow keys to highlight the category you
   want to delete.

4. Press Ctrl-D.

5. Press Enter to delete the category. Press Esc if you
   do not want to delete the category.

To delete classes

1. Press **Alt-S**-Shortcuts from the Register or Write Checks screen.

2. Select **L**-Select/Set Up Class, or press **Ctrl-L**.

3. Use the arrow keys to highlight the class you want to delete.

4. Press **Ctrl-D**.

5. Press **Enter** to delete the class. Press **Esc** if you do not want to delete the class.

To delete accounts

1. Select **A**-Select Account from the Main menu.

2. Use the arrow keys to highlight the account you want to delete.

3. Press **Ctrl-D**.

4. Type **YES** and press **Enter** to delete the account. Press **Esc** if you do not want to delete the account.

To delete files

1. Select **P**-Set Preferences from the Main menu.

2. Select **F**-File Activities.

3. Select **S**-Select/Set Up File.

4. Use the arrow keys to highlight the name of the file you want to delete.

5. Press **Ctrl-D**.

6. Type **YES** and press **Enter** to delete the file. Press **Esc** if you do not want to delete the file.

Edit Account Information

Purpose

Renames accounts, changes account descriptions, or changes credit card limits.

Notes

If you are editing information on investment accounts, see *Investment Accounts*.

See also *Accounts*.

Edit Reports

Purpose

Enables you to edit reports as they are displayed on-screen.

To access the Edit menu from Report screens

1. Select C-Create Reports from the Main menu.

2. Select the report you want to create from the next two menus.

3. Quicken displays the report on your screen and a menu bar at the top of the screen.

4. Press Alt-E-Edit to display the Edit pull-down menu.

Edit options available from the Edit pull-down menu

D-Set Title & Date Range option enables you to change the title and the date range of the report while the report is displayed.

F-Filter Transactions option enables you to change the report filter criteria while the report is displayed.

A-Accounts option enables you to limit the accounts Quicken uses to generate the report to Current, All, or Selected.

C-Categories option enables you to limit the categories Quicken uses to generate the report to Selected, All, or Tax-Related Only.

L-Classes option enables you to limit the classes used to generate the report to Selected or All.

Note

See also *Report Options*, *Filters*, and *Printing Reports*.

Examine Report Detail

Purpose

Enables you to view the transaction detail behind a report entry using the QuickZoom option.

Note

See *QuickZoom*.

Expand Reports

Purpose

Returns collapsed report detail to its original format.

To expand a report

1. With the report displayed on-screen, use the arrow keys to position the cursor on the row heading you want to expand.

2. Press Alt-L-Layout.

3. Select X-Expand, or press +.

4. Quicken displays the detail for the row heading.

Notes

The Collapse and Expand features are available only for Summary, Budget, or Account Balances reports.

See *Collapse Reports*.

Exporting Data

Purpose

Exports transactions, categories and classes, accounts, and memorized transactions into an ASCII file.

To export transactions from the Write Checks screen or the Register

1. Select W-Write/Print Checks or R-Use Register from the Main menu.

2. Press Alt-P-Print/Acct.

3. Select E-Export.

4. Type the name of the file to receive the data. You can enter a full pathname to specify any file.

5. Type the starting and ending dates of transactions you want to include in the export procedure. All the dates you type are inclusive.

6. Press Y at the Export Transactions blank.

7. Press Enter or F10 to export your Quicken transaction data.

To export categories and classes

1. Select W-Write/Print Checks or R-Use Register from the Main menu.

2. Press Alt-P-Print/Acct.

3. Select E-Export.

4. Type the name of the file to receive the data. You can enter a full pathname to specify any file.

5. Type the starting and ending dates of transactions you want to include in the export procedure. All the dates you type are inclusive.

6. Press Y at the Export Categories and Classes blank.

7. Press Enter or F10 to export your Quicken category and class data.

To export accounts

1. Select W-Write/Print Checks or R-Use Register from the Main menu.

2. Press Alt-P-Print/Acct.

3. Select E-Export.

4. Type the name of the file to receive the data. You can enter a full pathname to specify any file.

5. Type the starting and ending dates of transactions you want to include in the export procedure. All the dates you type are inclusive.

6. Press **Y** at the Export Accounts blank.

7. Press **Enter** or **F10** to export your Quicken account data.

To export memorized transactions

1. Select **W**-Write/Print Checks or **R**-Use Register from the Main menu.

2. Press **Alt-P**-Print/Acct.

3. Select **E**-Export.

4. Type the name of the file to receive the data. You can enter a full pathname to specify any file.

5. Type the starting and ending dates of transactions you want to include in the export procedure. All the dates you type are inclusive.

6. Press **Y** at the Export Memorized Transactions blank.

7. Press **Enter** or **F10** to export your Quicken memorized transaction data.

File Activities

Purpose

Sets up files of similar accounts so that you can separate the tasks you perform using Quicken.

To select the File Activities menu

1. Select **P**-Set Preferences from the Main menu.

2. Select **F**-File Activities.

To create a new file

1. Select **P**-Set Preferences from the Main menu.

2. Select **F**-File Activities.

3. Select **S**-Select/Set Up File.

4. Use the arrow keys to highlight the `<Set Up File>` line. Press **Enter**.

5. Enter a DOS file name (up to eight characters long) at the Set Up File window to use for the new file.

6. Specify the location of the new file by entering the drive and pathname. Press Enter.

7. Indicate what standard categories you want to use.

   Press 1 to use the predefined home categories.
   Press 2 to use the business categories.
   Press 3 to use both home and business categories.
   Press 4 to use none of the standard categories.

8. Press Enter.

To change from one file to another

1. Select P-Set Preferences from the Main menu.

2. Select F-File Activities.

3. Select S-Select/Set Up File.

4. Use the arrow keys to highlight the name of the file you want to use. Press Enter.

5. From the Select File To Use window, select the file with which you want to work.

6. Press Enter.

To delete a file

1. Select P-Set Preferences from the Main menu.

2. Select F-File Activities.

3. Select S-Select/Set Up File.

4. Use the arrow keys to highlight the file you want to delete.

5. Press Ctrl-D to delete the file.

6. Type YES to confirm deletion of the file. Press Enter.

   Quicken removes the file permanently.

To back up a file

1. Select P-Set Preferences from the Main menu.

2. Select F-File Activities.

3. Select B-Back Up File.

4. Type the drive letter for the floppy disk to which you are backing up the file. Make sure that the disk is in the drive and press Enter.

5. Use the arrow keys to select the file you want to back up. Press Enter.

To restore a file

1. Select P-Set Preferences from the Main menu.

2. Select F-File Activities.

3. Select R-Restore File.

4. Insert the floppy disk into the drive from which you will restore the data. Type the letter of the drive and press Enter.

5. Use the arrow keys to select the file you want to restore. Press Enter.

   Quicken restores the accounts to your hard drive in the file contained on the backup disk.

To copy a file

1. Select P-Set Preferences to make sure that the file you want to copy is active.

2. Select F-File Activities.

3. Select S-Select/Set Up File.

4. Use the arrow keys to select the file you want to use. Press Enter.

5. Press Esc to return to the File Activities menu.

6. Select C-Copy File from the File Activities menu.

7. Type the DOS file name for the new file in the Copy File window. Press Enter.

8. Type the path where the new file will be located and press Enter.

9. Type the beginning and ending dates for transactions you want to copy and press Enter, or simply press Enter to accept the default date range.

10. Press Y to copy prior uncleared transactions and press Enter.

11. Press **Y** to copy all investment transactions.

12. Press **Enter** to start the copy procedure.

13. Press **1** to reload the original file, or press **2** to load the file you just copied.

To change where Quicken looks for data

1. Select **P**-Set Preferences from the Main menu.

2. Select **F**-File Activities.

3. Select **L**-Set File Location.

4. Type the name of a new directory or drive.

5. Press **Enter**.

To perform year end file activities

1. Select **P**-Set Preferences from the Main menu.

2. Select **F**-File Activities.

3. Select **Y**-Year End.

4. Quicken displays the Year End window. Press **1** to select the Archive option, or press **2** to select the Start New Year option.

5. Enter information as prompted in the screens that follow.

Note

See also *Year End File Activities*.

Filters

Purpose

Defines which transactions your reports include.

To reset all filter settings

1. Press **F9**-Filter from the Create Report window.

2. Press **Ctrl-D**-Reset.

3. Press **Enter** to reset the filter settings to the default settings.

To set a filter for Personal and Business reports

1. Press **F9**-Filter from any Create Report window. Quicken displays the Filter Report Transactions window.

2. Enter values in any of the four blanks of the Restrict Report To Transactions Meeting These Criteria window.

   The report you generate will contain only information that matches what you have entered in the following four categories. If you don't want to specify a certain category, leave it blank.

   Enter the name of a payee in the Payee blank to report only those transactions with a specific Payee name.

   Enter information in the Memo blank to report only those transactions with a specific memo in the Register or Check Printing screen.

   Enter a category name to report only those transactions assigned to a specific category name.

   You can type the category name, or press **Ctrl-C** to select from the Category List.

   Enter a class name to report only transactions with a specific class name.

   You can type the class name, or press **Ctrl-L** to select from the Class List.

3. Press **Y** at the Select Categories To Include blank if you want to select the categories your report includes.

4. Press **Y** at the Select Classes To Include In The Report blank if you want to select the classes your report includes.

5. Press **Y** at the Tax-Related Categories Only blank if you want to report on tax-related categories.

6. Type **B**, **E**, or **A** at the next blank to indicate whether you want to restrict transactions in a report to amounts below, equal to, or above a certain amount. Enter the amount you want the transactions to be restricted below, equal to, or above.

7. Press **P** at the Payments/Deposits/Unprinted Checks/ All blank to restrict the report to payments. Press **D** to restrict it to deposits. Press **U** to restrict it to unprinted checks. Press **A** to include all types of transactions.

8. Press **Y** at the Cleared Status Is blank to report on transactions with a specific cleared status.

9. Continue generating your report as usual.

Finding Transactions

Purpose

Locates specific transactions in the Register.

To find a transaction in the Register

1. Select **R**-Use Register from the Main menu.

2. Press **Alt-E**-Edit.

3. Select **F**-Find, or press **Ctrl-F**.

4. Press **Ctrl-D** to clear the Transaction To Find window.

5. Type a word, number, or phrase for which you want to search. You can specify the check number, payee, memo line, category, payment amount, or deposit amount.

   Be accurate when filling in this blank; Quicken will search for exactly what you have entered in this blank.

6. Press **Ctrl-N** to search forward in the Register or **Ctrl-B** to search backward through your transactions.

7. Continue pressing **Ctrl-N** or **Ctrl-B** to find all transactions with the specified search criteria.

To find a transaction in the Write Checks screen

1. Select **W**-Write/Print Checks from the Main menu.

2. Press **Alt-E**-Edit.

3. Select **F**-Find, or press **Ctrl-F**.

4. Press **Ctrl-D** to clear the Transaction To Find window.

5. Type a word, number, or phrase for which you want to search. You can specify the check number, payee, memo line, category, payment amount, or deposit amount. Be accurate when filling in this blank.

6. Press Ctrl-N to search forward in the Register or Ctrl-B to search backward through your transactions.

7. Continue pressing Ctrl-N or Ctrl-B to find all transactions with the specified search criteria.

Function Keys

Purpose

Simplifies making menu choices using the function-key menu style.

Function keys at the Main menu

Key	Action
F1	Receives context-sensitive Help
F2	Accesses the Write Checks screen
F3	Displays menu of reports to generate
F4	Displays the Select Account To Use screen
F5	Accesses the Set Preferences menu
F6	Accesses the Tutorials and Assistants menu
F10	Emulates pressing Enter

Function keys at the Write Checks screen or the Register

Key	Action
F1	Displays context-sensitive Help
F2	Pulls down the Print/Acct menu
F3	Pulls down the Edit menu
F4	Pulls down the Shortcuts menu

Key	Action
F5	Pulls down the Reports menu
F6	Pulls down the Activities menu
F10	Enters a transaction or records a check in the Register

Go To Date

Purpose

Locates a specific date.

To find a specific date in the Write Checks screen or Register

1. Select W-Write/Print Checks or R-Use Register from the Main menu.

2. Press Alt-E-Edit.

3. Select G-Go to Date, or press Ctrl-G.

4. Type the date of the transaction you want to find. Press Enter.

   If there is no transaction on the specified date, Quicken finds the date that is closest to the one you enter.

Handwritten Checks

Purpose

Keeps track of your regular handwritten bank checks in the Register.

To enter a handwritten check in the Register

1. Select A-Select Account from the Main menu.

2. Use the arrow keys to highlight your checking account. Press Enter.

3. Press End to highlight the next empty blank in the Register.

4. Enter the date of the handwritten check in the Date column.

5. Enter the check number in the Num blank.

6. Type the name of the payee in the Payee blank.

7. Enter the transaction amount in the Payment blank if it represents a withdrawal from your account.

8. Enter an optional comment line at the Memo blank.

9. Enter the category and/or class to which you want to assign the transaction. You can either type the category or class in the Category blank or press Ctrl-C to choose from a list of category and/or class names.

10. Press Ctrl-Enter or F10 to record the transaction into your Quicken checking account Register.

Help System

Purpose

Provides context-sensitive information from almost anywhere within the program.

To access the Help system

1. Press F1-Help from anywhere in the program for information about the current screen, window, or menu.

2. Press ↓ or PgDn to scroll Help messages that are too long to fit in the Help window.

3. Press Ctrl-F1 to display a Help Index with a list of all available Help topics.

4. Use the arrow keys to highlight a topic from the Help Index. Press Enter to see more information on the topic.

5. Press F1 twice to display a Table of Contents that lists Help topics by task.

6. Use the arrow keys to highlight a topic from the Table of Contents and press Enter to see more information on the topic.

7. Use Tab to move to a bold phrase within a Help window, and press Enter to see more information on the phrase.

8. Press Esc when you want to exit Help.

Home Categories

Purpose

Identifies specific types of transactions that are used in your personal finances.

Standard Home Categories

The following chart lists the standard home categories that Quicken includes. The chart contains the category; its description; if it is a tax-related item; and its type.

Category	Description	Tax Rel	Type
Bonus	Bonus Income	*	Inc
Canada Pen	Canadian Pension	*	Inc
Div Income	Dividend Income	*	Inc
Gift Received	Gift Received	*	Inc
Int Inc	Interest Income	*	Inc
Invest Inc	Investment Income	*	Inc
Old Age Pension	Old Age Pension	*	Inc
Other Inc	Other Income	*	Inc
Salary	Salary Income	*	Inc
Auto	Automobile Expenses		Expns
Fuel	Automobile Fuel		Expns
Loan	Auto Loan Payment		Expns
Service	Auto Service		Expns
Bank Chrg	Bank Charge		Expns
Charity	Charitable Donations	*	Expns

Childcare	Childcare Expense		Expns
Christmas	Christmas Expenses		Expns
Clothing	Clothing		Expns
Dining	Dining Out		Expns
Dues	Dues		Expns
Education	Education		Expns
Entertain	Entertainment		Expns
Gifts	Gift Expenses		Expns
Groceries	Groceries		Expns
Home Rpair	Home Repair & Maint.		Expns
Household	Household Misc. Expenses		Expns
Housing	Housing		Expns
Insurance	Insurance		Expns
Int Exp	Interest Expense	*	Expns
Invest Exp	Investment Expense	*	Expns
Medical	Medical & Dental	*	Expns
Misc	Miscellaneous		Expns
Mort Int	Mortgage Interest Expense	*	Expns
Other Exp	Other Expenses		Expns
Recreation	Recreation Expense		Expns
RRSP	Regular Retirement Savings Plan		Expns
Subscriptions	Subscriptions		Expns

Category	Description	Tax Rel	Type
Supplies	Supplies		Expns
Tax	Taxes	*	Expns
Fed	Federal Tax	*	Expns
FICA	Social Security Tax	*	Expns
Other	Misc. Taxes	*	Expns
Prop	Property Tax	*	Expns
State	State Tax	*	Expns
Telephone	Telephone Expense		Expns
UIC	Unemployment Insurance Commission	*	Expns
Utilities	Utilities		Expns
Gas & Electric	Electric		Expns
Water	Water		Expns

Note

See also *Categories*.

Important Keys

Purpose

Helps you move within the program and accomplish more in less time.

Editing transactions in checks and window entries

Key(s)	Action
Del	Deletes character at cursor
Backspace	Deletes character to left of cursor

Ctrl-Backspace	Deletes entire entry in blank
Tab	Moves to next blank
Shift-Tab	Moves to previous blank
Ctrl-→	Moves to next word
Ctrl-←	Moves to previous word
Enter	Records transaction and closes window
Ins	Switches between Insert and Overtype mode

Register keystrokes

Key(s)	Action
↓	Moves to next transaction
↑	Moves to previous transaction
PgDn	Moves down one screen
PgUp	Moves up one screen
Ctrl-PgDn	Moves to first transaction in next month
Ctrl-PgUp	Moves to first transaction in previous month
Home	Beginning of current blank
End	End of current blank
Home	Beginning of first blank
End	End of last blank
Ctrl-Home	First transaction in Register
Ctrl-End	Last transaction in Register

Special characters in Filter Transactions/Find windows

Character(s)	Action
..	Matches any text
~	Excludes transactions

Character(s)	Action
?	Substitutes for a single character
=	Matches exactly

Special characters in the Register/Write Checks screen

Character(s)	Action
/	Separates categories from classes
:	Separates categories from subcategories; separates classes from subclasses
>>>>>	Signifies an untransmitted electronic payment
X	Signifies a cleared transaction

Importing Data

Purpose

Imports data from an ASCII file into a Quicken file.

To import transactions from a file to the Write Checks screen

1. Select **W**-Write/Print Checks from the Main menu.
2. Press **Alt-P**-Print/Acct.
3. Select **I**-Import.
4. Type the file name from which the data will be imported. You can enter a full pathname to specify any file.
5. Type **Y** to include items that are transfers from another Quicken account. Type **N** to not include transfers.
6. Press **Enter** or **F10** to import the transactions.

To import transactions from an ASCII file to the Register

1. Select **R**-Use Register from the Main menu.
2. Press **Alt-P**-Print/Acct.
3. Select **I**-Import.

4. Type the file name from which the data will be imported. You can enter a full pathname to specify any file.

5. Type **Y** to include items that are transfers from another Quicken account. Type **N** to not include transfers.

6. Press **Enter** or **F10** to import the transactions.

Investment Accounts

Purpose

Keeps track of investments in stocks, bonds, mutual funds, and other securities that fluctuate in price.

To set up a new investment account

1. Select **A**-Select Account from the Main menu.

2. Use the arrow keys or **Home** to highlight <New Account>. Press **Enter**.

3. Enter the investment account information in the Set Up New Account window.

4. Press **6** to select an investment account.

5. Type the account name in the Name For This Account blank.

6. If the account is a single mutual-fund investment account, type **Y** in the Account Is A Single Mutual Fund (Y/N) blank. Type **N** if the account is not.

7. Enter an optional account description, such as the institution where you have the account or the account number.

8. Fill in the Set Up Mutual Fund Security window, which appears if you are setting up a single mutual fund.

   The window asks for the following information:

   Name
   Symbol
   Type of investment
   Goal of the investment

9. Press **Ctrl-L** to select the type of investment from the Investment Type List. This list contains the following choices:

> Bond
> CD
> Mutual Fund
> Stock

Note that you can add a new security type to the list at any time.

10. Press **Ctrl-L** at the Goal field to access a list of investment goals. You can select from the following predetermined choices:

> College Fund
> Growth
> High Risk
> Income
> Low Risk

Note that you can add a new goal to the list at any time.

11. Press **Enter** or **F10** to set up the investment account.

To edit the name and description of an investment account

1. Select **A**-Select Account from the Main menu.

2. Use the arrow keys to highlight the account you want to modify. Press **Ctrl-E**.

3. Type the new account name and description in the Edit Account Information window.

4. Press **Enter** after you have made the necessary changes.

To delete an investment account

1. Select **A**-Select Account from the Main menu.

2. Use the arrow keys to highlight the account you want to delete. Press **Ctrl-D**.

3. Type **YES** to confirm deletion of the account.

4. Press **Enter**.

Types of investment accounts

Quicken uses two types of investment accounts: Regular and Mutual-Fund. A Regular Investment account has the following features:

- It contains one or more securities.

- Its Register displays the cash balance after every transaction.

A Mutual-Fund Investment account has the following features:

- It is restricted to one security.

- It has a zero cash balance.

- Its Register displays the total number of shares of the single security as well as the current market value of the security.

- The name of the security automatically appears in the Register.

Investment Actions

When you use investment accounts, you enter the information about them in the Register. You describe what is happening to the security in the Action column. In the Security column, you enter the name of the security.

Action Symbol	Action Description
Buy	Buy security with cash from account
BuyX	Buy security with cash transferred into account
CGLong	Receive cash from long-term capital gains
CGLongX	Transfer out of account cash received from long-term capital gains
CGShort	Receive cash from short-term capital gains

Action Symbol	Action Description
CGShortX	Transfer out of account cash received from short-term capital gains
Div	Receive cash from dividend
DivX	Transfer out of account cash received from interest
IntInc	Receive cash from interest income
MargInt	Pay for interest on margin loan by using cash from other account
MiscExp	Pay for expense using cash from other account
MiscInc	Receive cash from miscellaneous income
ReinvDiv	Reinvest in additional shares of security
ReinvInt	Reinvest in additional shares of the security with money from interest distribution
ReinvLg	Reinvest in additional shares of the security with money from long-term capital gains
ReinvSh	Reinvest in additional shares of the security
Reminder	Remind of some event associated with investment account
RtrnCap	Receive cash from return of capital
Sell	Sell security and leave cash in account
SellX	Sell security and transfer cash out of account
ShrsIn	Transfer shares into account
ShrsOut	Transfer shares out of account

StkSplit	Change number of shares due to stock split
Xin	Transfer cash into account
Xout	Transfer cash out of account

To add a security to the Security List

1. Select A-Select Account from the Main menu.

2. Use the arrow keys to select the investment account you want to use. Press Enter.

3. From the investment Register, press Alt-S-Shortcuts.

4. Select S-Security List, or press Ctrl-Y.

5. Press Home to select <New Security>.

6. Type the name of the new security and include the lot number if you will be tracking the security by lot.

7. Type the symbol for the security if you plan to import price data from another file.

8. At the Type field, press Ctrl-L to display the list of security types. Use the arrow keys to select a security type and press Enter.

9. At the Goal field, press Ctrl-L to display the list of investment goals. Use the arrow keys to select an investment goal and press Enter.

10. Press Enter or F10 to add the new security.

To add a new security type

1. Select A-Select Account from the Main menu.

2. Use the arrow keys to select the investment account you want to use. Press Enter.

3. From the investment Register, press Alt-S-Shortcuts.

4. Select S-Security List, or press Ctrl-Y.

5. Press Home to select <New Security>.

6. Type the name of the new security and include the lot number if you will be tracking the security by lot.

7. Type the symbol for the security if you plan to import price data from another file.

8. From the Type field of the Set Up Security window, press **Ctrl-L**.

9. Press **Home** to select `<Set Up New Type>`.

10. Type the name of the new security type.

11. Indicate how you want prices of this security type displayed. Press **1** to display prices in decimal format or **2** to display prices in fractional format.

12. Press **Enter** or **F10** to add the new security type.

To add a new investment goal

1. From the Main menu, select **A**-Select Account.

2. Use the arrow keys to select the investment account you want to use. Press **Enter**.

3. From the investment Register, press **Alt-S**-Shortcuts.

4. Select **S**-Security List, or press **Ctrl-Y**.

5. Press **Home** to select `<New Security>`.

6. Type the name of the new security and include the lot number if you will be tracking the security by lot.

7. Type the symbol for the security if you plan to import price data from another file.

8. From the Goal field of the investment Register, press **Ctrl-L**.

9. Press **Home** to select `<Set Up New Goal>`.

10. Type the name for your new goal.

11. Press **Enter** or **F10** to add the new investment goal.

To update prices of securities

1. From the Main menu, select **A**-Select Account.

2. Use the arrow keys to select the investment account you want to use. Press **Enter**.

3. Press **Alt-A**-Activities from the investment Register.

4. Select **U**-Update Prices, or press **Ctrl-U**.

5. Quicken displays the Update Prices and Market Value screen that lists the following for each security (listed alphabetically by type):

Type
Market Price
Average Cost
% Gain
Shares
Market Value

6. Press **F8** if you want to combine lots of the same security on the Update Prices and Market Value screen.

7. Press **F9** to view the Update Prices and Market Value screen for All Accounts. Press **F9** again to return to the screen for One Account.

8. Use ↑ and ↓ to highlight the security you want to update.

9. Type the current market price of the security in the Market Price column. Use + and – to change market prices by increments of 1/8. An up or down arrow next to the market price indicates an increase or decrease in share price over the previous known share price.

10. Press **Ctrl-Enter** or **F10** to record prices.

To print the Update Prices and Market Value screen

1. From the Update Prices and Market Value screen, press **Ctrl-P**.

2. Enter the number of the printer you want to use if it is different from the default.

3. Press **Enter** or **F10** to print the screen.

To adjust the cash balance in an investment account

1. Select **A**-Select Account from the Main menu.

2. Use the arrow keys to select the investment account you want to use and press **Enter**.

3. From the investment Register, press **Alt-A**-Activities.

4. Select **A**-Adjust Balance.

5. Press **1**-Adjust Cash Balance.

6. Type the adjusted cash balance from your account statement and press **Enter**.

7. Type the adjustment date.

8. Press **Ctrl-Enter** to record the adjustment in the investment Register.

To adjust the share balance in an investment account

1. Select **A**-Select Account from the Main menu.

2. Use the arrow keys to select the investment account you want to use and press **Enter**.

3. From the investment Register, press **Alt-A**-Activities.

4. Select **A**-Adjust Balance.

5. Press **2**-Adjust Share Balance.

6. Type the adjustment date and press **Enter**.

7. At the Security To Adjust blank, press **Ctrl-Y** to display the list of securities.

8. Use the arrow keys to select a security and press **Enter**.

9. Type the adjusted share balance from your account statement for this security.

10. Press **Ctrl-Enter** to record the adjustment in the investment Register.

Note

You can memorize recurring investment transactions, such as the receipt of quarterly dividends. See *Memorizing Transactions*.

═ **Investment Income Report** ═

Purpose

Shows interest income, divided income, capital gains distributions, realized gains and losses, and margin interest and other investment expense for a specified time period.

To generate an Investment Income report

1. Select **C**-Create Reports from the Main menu.

2. Select I-Investment Reports.

3. Select I-Investment Income Report.

4. Enter an optional report title. Press Enter.

5. Enter the dates between which you want to restrict transactions.

6. Type the number that corresponds to the desired method for subtotalling the report.

7. Press C if you want to include the current investment account in the report. Press A to include all investment accounts. Press S to include selected investment accounts in the report.

8. Press Enter.

9. Preview the report displayed on the screen; use the arrow keys to scroll the display.

10. Press Ctrl-P-Print when you are ready to print.

11. Enter the number of the printer you want to use if it is different from the default.

12. Press Enter or F10 to print the report.

To set report options

1. Select C-Create Reports from the Main menu.

2. Select I-Investment Reports.

3. Select I-Investment Income Report.

4. Press F8-Options.

5. Press 1 if you want to report income and expense. Press 2 if you want to report on a cash flow basis.

6. Press the number that corresponds to the desired method for handling transfers.

7. Press Y if you want to show cents when displaying amounts. Press N if you do not want to show cents.

8. Press Enter or F10 to create the report.

Note

See also *Filters*.

Investment Performance Report

Purpose

Shows the average annual return of your securities during a specified time period.

To generate an Investment Performance report

1. Select C-Create Reports from the Main menu.

2. Select I-Investment Reports.

3. Select P-Investment Performance Report.

4. Enter an optional title. Press Enter.

5. Type the number that corresponds to the desired method for subtotalling the report.

6. Press Y at the next blank to show transaction details in your report.

7. Press C if you want to include the current investment account in the report. Press A to include all investment accounts in the report. Press S to include selected investment accounts.

8. Press Ctrl-P-Print when you are ready to print the report.

9. Type the number of the printer you want to use if it is different from the default.

10. Press Enter or F10 to print the report.

To define how dollar amounts are displayed

1. Select C-Create Reports from the Main menu.

2. Select I-Investment Reports.

3. Select P-Investment Performance Report.

4. Press F8-Options.

5. Press Y if you want to show cents when displaying amounts. Press N if you do not want to show cents.

6. Press Enter to return to the previous window.

Note

See also *Filters* and *Printing*.

Investment Transactions Report

Purpose

Shows how transactions during a specified time period have affected either the market value or the cost basis of your investments.

To generate an Investment Transaction report

1. Select C-Create Reports from the Main menu.

2. Select I-Investment Reports.

3. Select T-Investment Transaction Report.

4. Enter an optional report title. Press Enter.

5. Enter the dates between which you want to restrict transactions.

6. Type the number that corresponds to the desired method for subtotalling the report.

7. Press C to include the current investment account in the report. Press A to include all investment accounts. Press S to include selected investment accounts.

8. Press Enter.

9. Preview the report that is displayed on your screen; use the arrow keys to scroll the display.

10. Press Ctrl-P-Print when you are ready to print.

11. Enter the number of the printer you want to use if it is different from the default.

12. Press Enter or F10 to print the report.

To set report options

1. Select C-Create Reports from the Main menu.

2. Select I-Investment Reports.

3. Select **T**-Investment Transaction Report.

4. Press **F8**-Options.

   The Report Options window appears.

5. Press **1** to report income and expense. Press **2** to report on a cash flow basis.

6. Press the number that corresponds to the desired method for handling transfers.

7. Press **Y** if you want to show cents when displaying amounts. Press **N** if you do not want to show cents.

8. Press **Enter** to return to the previous window.

Note

See also *Filters* and *Printing*.

Itemized Categories Personal Report

Purpose

Displays all the transactions in your accounts, grouped and subtotalled by category.

To generate an Itemized Categories report

1. Select **C**-Create Reports from the Main menu.

2. Select **P**-Personal Reports.

3. Select **I**-Itemized Categories.

4. Enter an optional report title and press **Enter**.

5. Enter the months between which you want to include transactions in the report. Press **Enter**.

6. Preview the report displayed on the screen; use the arrow keys to scroll the display.

7. Press **Ctrl-P**-Print when you are ready to print the report.

8. Enter the number of the printer you want to use if it is different from the default.

9. Press **Enter** or **F10** to print the report.

Note

See also *Customize Report* and *Filters*.

Job/Project Business Report

Purpose

Summarizes your income and expenses by class.

To create a Job/Project report

1. Select **C**-Create Reports from the Main menu.

2. Select **B**-Business Reports.

3. Select **J**-Job/Project Report.

4. Type an optional title. Press **Enter**.

5. Preview the report displayed on the screen; use the arrow keys to scroll the display.

6. Press **Ctrl-P**-Print when you are ready to print the report.

7. Enter the number of the printer you want to use if it is different from the default.

8. Press **Enter** or **F10** to print the report.

Note

See also *Customize Report* and *Filters*.

Loan Calculator

Purpose

Amortizes loans.

To use the loan calculator

1. Press **Alt-A**-Activities from the Write Checks screen or the Register.

2. Press **L**-Loan Calculator.

3. Type the principal amount of the loan, the annual interest rate (up to four decimal places), the total years (period of time the loan covers), and the number of periods (payments) per year. Press **Enter**.

4. Quicken calculates the payment amount and displays it in the Regular Payment = field at the bottom of the calculator.

5. Press **Esc** to clear the loan calculator from the screen.

To view the loan payment schedule

1. Press **Alt-A**-Activities from the Write Checks screen or the Register.

2. Press **L**-Loan Calculator.

3. Type the principal amount of the loan, the annual interest rate (up to four decimal places), the total years (period of time the loan covers), and the number of periods (payments) per year. Press **Enter**.

4. Quicken calculates the payment amount and displays it in the Regular Payment = field at the bottom of the calculator.

5. Press **F9**. Scroll up and down the Approximate Payment Schedule window to view the entire payment schedule.

6. Press **Esc** to remove the payment schedule from the screen.

To print the loan payment schedule

1. Press **Alt-A**-Activities from the Write Checks screen or the Register.

2. Press **L**-Loan Calculator.

3. Type the principal amount of the loan, the annual interest rate (up to four decimal places), the total years (period of time the loan covers), and the number of periods (payments) per year. Press **Enter**.

4. Quicken calculates the payment amount and displays it in the Regular Payment = field at the bottom of the calculator.

5. Press **F9** to display the Approximate Payment Schedule window.

6. Press **Ctrl-P**.

7. Enter the number of the printer you are using if it is different from the default.

8. Press **Enter** or **F10** to begin printing.

Marking Transactions

Purpose

Clears transactions within Quicken that your bank has processed.

To mark a single transaction as cleared

1. Select either **W**-Write/Print Checks or **R**-Use Register from the Main menu.

2. Press **Alt**-**A**-Activities.

3. Select **E**-Reconcile to start the reconciling process.

4. Enter the information in the Reconcile Register With Bank Statement window. Press **Ctrl-Enter** to display the list of uncleared transactions.

5. Use ↑ and ↓ to highlight the transaction you want to mark as cleared.

6. Press **Enter** to mark the transaction as cleared.

7. Press **F9** to view the Register to make any necessary changes.

8. Continue reconciling your account as usual.

To mark a range of transactions as cleared

1. Select either **W**-Write/Print Checks or **R**-Use Register from the Main menu.

2. Press **Alt**-**A**-Activities.

3. Select **E**-Reconcile to start the reconciling process.

4. Enter the information in the Reconcile Register With Bank Statement window. Press **Ctrl-Enter** to display the list of uncleared transactions.

5. Press **F8**-Mark Range.

6. Enter the range of checks that have cleared in the Mark Range of Check Numbers as Cleared window and press **Enter**.

7. Continue reconciling your account as usual.

Memorized Reports

Purpose

Standardizes reports by using the same report instructions each time you generate a certain report.

To memorize a report

1. Select **C**-Create Reports from the Main menu or **Alt-R**-Reports from the Register or the Write Checks screen.

2. Select the type of report you want to create.

3. Fill in the blanks for the report you want to memorize.

4. Press **Ctrl-M** at the preview screen.

   Quicken prompts you for a title for your memorized report. Quicken then beeps twice to confirm your memorized report.

To recall a memorized report

1. Select **C**-Create Reports from the Main menu or **Alt-R**-Reports from the Register or the Write Checks screen.

2. Select **M**-Memorized Reports.

3. Use the arrow keys to select the report you want to use from the list of memorized reports. Press **Enter**.

4. Enter changes to the report criteria displayed on your screen or continue printing the report as usual.

To delete a memorized report

1. Select **C**-Create Reports from the Main menu or **Alt-R**-Reports from the Register or the Write Checks screen.

2. Select **M**-Memorized Reports.

3. Use the arrow keys to highlight the report you want to delete. Press **Ctrl-D**.

To rename a memorized report

1. Select **C**-Create Reports from the Main menu or **Alt-R**-Reports from the Register or the Write Checks screen.

2. Select **M**-Memorized Reports.

3. Use the arrow keys to select the report you want to rename. Press **Ctrl-E**.

4. Type the new name. Press **Enter**.

Memorizing Transactions

Purpose

Stores check or register transactions that are entered in your accounts.

To memorize a transaction

1. Select **W**-Write/Print Checks or **R**-Use Register from the Main menu.

2. Enter the information you want memorized in the Write Checks screen or the Register.

3. Press **Alt-S**-Shortcuts.

4. Select **M**-Memorize Transaction, or press **Ctrl-M**.

5. Quicken highlights the information you want memorized. Press **Enter** to confirm that you want the information memorized.

   You are returned to the Write Checks screen or the Register, wherever you were when you started.

6. To complete the transaction you have just entered, press **Ctrl-Enter** or **F10**. If you do not want to record the transaction in the Write Checks screen or the Register, press **Ctrl-D**.

To memorize a loan payment

1. Select W-Write/Print Checks or R-Use Register from the Main menu.

2. Highlight the loan payment transaction you want to memorize.

3. Press Alt-S-Shortcuts.

4. Select M-Memorize Transaction, or press Ctrl-M.

5. Quicken highlights the information you want memorized. Press Enter to confirm that you want the information memorized.

    You are returned to the Write Checks screen or the Register, wherever you were when you started.

6. Press Ctrl-T to display the Memorized Transactions List.

7. Highlight the loan payment you just memorized and press F9-Amortize.

8. Type the payment amount, annual interest rate, loan period (in years), and the number of periods per year. Note that Quicken calculates the approximate loan amount.

9. Type the payee name, optional memo, the category name for the principal portion of the loan payment, and the category name for the interest portion of the loan payment.

10. Type the date of the first loan payment and the number of payments made to date.

11. Press F9 to view the amortization schedule.

12. Press Enter twice to add the amortized loan payment to the Memorized Transactions List. Note that memorized loan payments are designated by an A in the Split column of the list.

To memorize an address of a payee

1. Select W-Write/Print Checks or R-Use Register from the Main menu.

2. Press Alt-S-Shortcuts.

3. Select **R**-Recall Transactions, or press **Ctrl-T**.

4. At the Memorized Transactions List, press **Home** to highlight the <New Transaction> line and press **Enter**.

5. Type the transaction information you want to memorize, and then press **F8** to display the Memorized Transaction Address window.

6. Fill in the address and an optional message, and then press **Ctrl-Enter**.

7. Each time you recall this memorized transaction at the Write Checks screen, Quicken will fill in the address automatically.

To recall a memorized transaction

1. Select **W**-Write/Print Checks or **R**-Use Register from the Main menu.

2. Press **Alt-S**-Shortcuts.

3. Select **R**-Recall Transaction, or press **Ctrl-T**.

4. At the Memorized Transactions List, use the arrow keys to highlight the memorized transaction you want to recall. Press **Enter**.

5. Add any necessary information to the recalled transaction after it appears on the Write Checks screen or the Register.

6. Press **Ctrl-Enter** or **F10** to record your modifications.

To add a transaction to the Memorized Transactions List

1. Select **W**-Write/Print Checks or **R**-Use Register from the Main menu.

2. Press **Alt-S**-Shortcuts.

3. Select **R**-Recall Transactions, or press **Ctrl-T**.

4. At the Memorized Transactions List, press **Home** to highlight the <New Transaction> line and press **Enter**.

5. Type the transaction information in the Edit/Setup Memorized Transaction window.

6. Press **F9** to specify whether the added transaction is a Payment, Check, Electronic Payment, or a Deposit. Press **Enter** to return to the Edit/Setup Memorized Transaction window.

7. Press **F10** to add the transaction to the Memorized Transactions List.

To edit a memorized transaction

1. Select **W**-Write/Print Checks or **R**-Use Register from the Main menu.

2. Press **Ctrl-T**.

3. Use the arrow keys to highlight the transaction you want to edit. Press **Ctrl-E**.

4. Make any necessary changes to the transaction in the Edit/Setup Memorized Transaction window.

5. Press **F10** to save the changes to the memorized transaction.

To delete a memorized transaction

1. Select **W**-Write/Print Checks or **R**-Use Register from the Main menu.

2. Press **Ctrl-T** to view the Memorized Transactions List.

3. Use the arrow keys to highlight the transaction you want to delete. Press **Ctrl-D**.

4. Press **Enter** to delete the memorized transaction.

To print the Memorized Transactions List

1. Select **W**-Write/Print Checks or **R**-Use Register from the Main menu.

2. Press **Ctrl-T** to view the Memorized Transactions List.

3. Press **Ctrl-P** when you are ready to print the Memorized Transactions List.

4. Type the number that corresponds to your printer if it is different from the default.

5. Press **Enter** or **F10** to begin printing.

Note

> With Quicken 5, you can memorize the amortization schedule for loan payments. Each time you make a payment on a loan, Quicken records the principal and interest amounts and allocates them to the proper categories.

Menu Styles

Purpose

> Provides two different menu styles for displaying menus and making menu selections: Alt-key and function-key.

To change the menu style from Alt-key to function-key

1. Select **P**-Set Preferences from the Main menu.

2. Select **S**-Screen Settings.

3. Select **A**-Menu Access.

4. Press **1**-Function-keys and press **Enter**.

5. The menu style will not change until you exit Quicken and restart the program.

To change the menu style from function-key to Alt-key

1. Select **5**-Set Preferences from the Main menu.

2. Select **3**-Screen Settings.

3. Select **4**-Menu Access.

4. Press **2**-Alt-keys and press **Enter**.

5. The menu style will not change until you exit Quicken and restart the program.

Note

> This Quick Reference uses the Alt-key menu style to explain commands.

Missing Check Business Report

Purpose

Lists transactions in the current account in check number order.

To generate a Missing Check report

1. Select C-Create Reports from the Main menu.

2. Select B-Business Reports.

3. Select M-Missing Check.

4. Type a title and press Enter. (This step is optional.)

5. Type the starting and ending dates for the report and press Enter.

6. Preview the report by using the arrow keys to scroll the display.

7. Press Ctrl-P-Print when you are ready to print the report.

8. Enter the number of the printer you want to use if it is different from the default.

9. Press Enter or F10 to print the report.

Notes

The Missing Check report lists an interruption in check number sequence as a `Missing Check`.

See *Printing Reports*.

Missing Check Personal Report

Purpose

Lists transactions in the current account in check number order.

To generate a Missing Check report

1. Select C-Create Reports from the Main menu.

2. Select P-Personal Reports.

3. Select **M**-Missing Check.

4. Type a title and press **Enter**. (This step is optional.)

5. Type the starting and ending dates for the report and press **Enter**.

6. Preview the report by using the arrow keys to scroll the display.

7. Press **Ctrl-P**-Print when you are ready to print the report.

8. Enter the number of the printer you want to use if it is different from the default.

9. Press **Enter** or **F10** to print the report.

Notes

The Missing Check report lists an interruption in check number sequence as a `Missing Check`.

See *Printing Reports*.

Monitor Display

Purpose

Enables you to adjust monitor settings that change the way Quicken displays information.

To change the screen colors

1. Select **P**-Set Preferences from the Main menu.

2. Select **S**-Screen Settings.

3. Select **C**-Screen Colors.

4. Type the number that corresponds to the color combination you prefer.

5. Press **Enter**.

To change the register and report display format

1. Select **P**-Set Preferences from the Main menu.

2. Select **S**-Screen Settings.

3. Select **D**-EGA/VGA 43 Line Display.

4. Type 2 to change to a compressed format (43 lines). The default format setting is 25 lines.

5. Press Enter.

To change the monitor speed

1. Select P-Set Preferences from the Main menu.

2. Select S-Screen Settings.

3. Select M-Monitor Display.

Monthly Budget Personal Report

Purpose

Compares the amount you have received or spent in each category with the amount you have budgeted.

To generate a Monthly Budget report

1. Select C-Create Reports from the Main menu.

2. Select P-Personal Reports.

3. Select B-Monthly Budget.

4. Enter a title for the report.

5. Enter the dates you want the report to cover. Press Enter.

6. Select F8-Options to customize the report or F9-Filter to set transaction filters.

7. Preview the report displayed on the screen; use the arrow keys to scroll the display.

8. Press Ctrl-P-Print when you are ready to print the report.

9. Enter the number of the printer you want to use if it is different from the default.

10. Press Enter or F10 to print the report.

Notes

This report includes all bank, cash, and credit card accounts. You set and change budget amounts for each of your categories while creating your Monthly Budget Personal report.

See also *Customize Report* and *Filters*.

Ordering Supplies

Purpose

Enables you to order the supplies you need to print checks with Quicken, or to order custom logos or the Quicken 5 Transfer Utility.

To print an order form

1. Select W-Write/Print Checks or R-Use Register from the Main menu.

2. Press Alt-A-Activities.

3. Select S-Order Supplies.

4. Select from the Print Supply Order Form window the number of the printer you want to use.

5. Make sure that your printer is turned on, loaded with paper, and on-line.

6. Press Enter to begin printing. Use the form Quicken prints to order available supplies.

Note

Quicken checks are ordered through the manufacturer. The checks are designed to work with Quicken software and your computer's printer.

P & L Statement Business Report

Purpose

Summarizes category-by-category income and expenses for all the accounts in your current file.

To print a Profit and Loss statement

1. Select C-Create Reports from the Main menu.

2. Select B-Business Reports.

3. Select S-P & L Statement.

4. Enter an optional title and press Enter. To customize the report, press F8-Options; to set transactions filters, press F9-Filter.

5. Preview the report that is displayed on your screen; use the arrow keys to scroll the display.

6. Press Ctrl-P-Print when you are ready to print the report.

7. Enter the number of the printer you want to use if it is different from the default.

8. Press Enter or F10 to print the report.

Note

See also *Customize Report* and *Filters*.

Password

Purpose

Prevents unauthorized access to your Quicken data.

To set the file password

1. Select P-Set Preferences from the Main menu.

2. Select W-Password Settings.

3. Select F-File Password.

4. Enter a maximum 16-character password.

5. Press Enter to create the password.

6. Confirm your password by reentering it at the prompt. Press Enter.

To change the file password

1. Select P-Set Preferences from the Main menu.

2. Select W-Password Settings.

3. Select **F**-File Password.

4. Enter your old password in the Change Password window and press **Enter**.

5. Enter your new password.

6. Press **Enter** to make the change.

7. Confirm your password by reentering it at the prompt. Press **Enter**.

To remove the file password

1. Select **P**-Set Preferences from the Main menu.

2. Select **W**-Password Settings.

3. Select **F**-File Password.

4. Enter your old password in the Change Password window and press **Enter**.

5. Press the **space bar** once at the New Password blank.

6. Press **Enter**.

To set the transaction password

1. Select **P**-Set Preferences from the Main menu.

2. Select **W**-Password Settings.

3. Select **T**-Transaction Password.

4. Enter a maximum 16-character password. Press **Enter**.

5. Type the date through which the password will be required.

6. Press **Enter**.

Notes

Quicken will accept lower- and uppercase characters in the password.

A transaction password requires you to enter a password before you can make changes to specified transactions. The transaction password permits others to view your Quicken records without changing them.

Make a note of your password. If you forget it, you will not be able to access the data in your Quicken file.

Paying Credit Card Bill

Purpose

Writes a check to pay your credit card bill.

To process your credit card statement

1. Select A-Select Account from the Main menu.

2. Use the arrow keys to select your credit card account. Press Enter.

3. Press Alt-A-Activities from the credit card Register.

4. Select E-Reconcile/Pay Credit Card to display the Credit Card Statement Information window.

5. Enter any new charges at the Charges, Cash Advances blank.

6. Enter the payments and credits listed on your statement.

7. Enter the ending balance shown on your statement.

8. Enter the finance charges for the month and the category to which the charges should be assigned in the last section of the Credit Card Statement Information window.

9. Press Enter. A new window appears that lists all uncleared items.

10. Use ↑ and ↓ to highlight each transaction that appears on your credit card statement.

11. Press Enter to mark transactions as cleared.

12. Press F8-Mark Range to mark several transactions in sequence as cleared. Enter the range of dates you want to mark as cleared and press Enter.

13. Compare the totals at the bottom of the screen with the totals printed on your credit card statement.

14. Continue to mark or unmark transactions until your credit card account is in balance.

15. Press **Ctrl-F10** when your credit card account is in balance. Quicken asks if you want to make a payment on the account.

16. In the Make Credit Card Payment window, type the name of the checking account to use to pay the credit card bill and press **Enter**.

17. Press **Y** to write a Quicken check, or press **N** to write a hand-written check.

18. Press **Enter** to process and record the payment in the check Register and the credit card Register, or press **Esc** if you do not want to pay the credit card bill now.

Payroll Business Report

Purpose

Reports on your payments to your employees and other payroll-related transactions.

To generate a Payroll report

1. Select **C**-Create Reports from the Main menu.

2. Select **B**-Business Reports.

3. Select **Y**-Payroll Report.

4. Enter a title. Press **Enter**. (This step is optional.)

5. Preview the report that is displayed on the screen; use the arrow keys to scroll the display.

6. Press **Ctrl-P**-Print when you are ready to print the report.

7. Enter the number of the printer you want to use if it is different from the default.

8. Press **Enter** or **F10** to begin printing.

Notes

The Payroll report has sections that total the gross payroll and payroll taxes for each employee, and the report shows transfer transactions in the accrued payroll liabilities accounts. Only transactions assigned to a category with the word *Payroll* are included in the report.

See also *Customize Report*, *Printing Reports*, and *Filters*.

Percentage Splits

Purpose

Enables you to assign a category to a percentage of the transaction total.

Note

See *Splitting Transactions*.

Personal Reports

Purpose

Reports on many common personal finance transactions.

To access the Personal Reports menu

1. Select C-Create Reports from the Main menu.

2. Select P-Personal Reports.

3. Select the report you want from the list of available personal reports.

Available Personal reports

Cash Flow Report

Totals the money you receive and spend each month by category.

Itemized Categories Report

Displays all the transactions in all your accounts sorted by category.

Monthly Budget Report

Compares on a month-by-month basis the actual amount you have received or spent in each category with the amount you have budgeted for each category.

Missing Check Report

Lists transactions in check number order and identifies any missing check numbers.

Net Worth Report

Presents the balances from all your accounts in the current file on a given date. Your net worth is calculated by subtracting total liabilities from total assets.

Tax Schedule Report

Lists transactions from all accounts that are assigned to categories with tax schedule information. The tax schedule report can be printed to a tax preparation software file, such as a TurboTax file.

Tax Summary Report

Similar to the Itemized Categories report, but it only includes transactions that are assigned to tax-related categories.

Notes

For information on generating a specific personal report, refer to the individual report name.

See also *Customize Report* and *Filters*.

Petty Cash

Purpose

Keeps detailed records of your cash transactions.

To create a Petty Cash account

1. Select A-Select Account from the Main menu.

2. Use the arrow keys or Home to highlight <New Account> from the Select Account To Use window. Press Enter.

3. Enter information about the new account in the Set Up New Account window.

4. Press 3 to select Cash Account as the type of account.

5. Enter the name of the new account in the Name For This Account blank.

6. Enter the amount of money you have on hand in the Balance blank.

7. Enter the date for which the beginning balance is valid.

8. Enter a description. (This step is optional.)

9. Press **Enter** or **F10** to create the new account.

Portfolio Value Report

Purpose

Shows the value of each of your securities on a specified date.

To generate a Portfolio Value report

1. Select **C**-Create Reports from the Main menu.

2. Select **I**-Investment Reports.

3. Select **V**-Portfolio Value.

4. Enter a title. Press **Enter**. (This step is optional.)

5. Enter the date for which you want the portfolio value.

6. Press **1** if you do not want the report subtotaled, **2** to subtotal by account, **3** to subtotal by security type, or **4** to subtotal by investment goal.

7. Press **C** to include the current investment account in the report. Press **A** to include all investment accounts. Press **S** to include selected investment accounts.

   If you press **S**, another window appears, listing your accounts. Select the accounts you want your report to include.

8. Press **Ctrl-P**-Print when you are ready to print the report.

9. Enter the number of the printer you want to use if it is different from the default.

10. Press **Enter** or **F10** to begin printing the report.

To tell Quicken how to report dollar amounts

1. Select **C**-Create Reports from the Main menu.

2. Select **I**-Investment Reports.

3. Select **V**-Portfolio Value.

4. Press **F8**-Options to display the Report Options window.

5. Press **Y** to show cents when displaying amounts. Press **N** to not show cents.

6. Press **Enter** to return to the previous window.

Note

See also *Filters*.

Positioning Checks in Your Printer

Purpose

Enables you to print sample checks to make sure that the checks are properly aligned in your printer before printing actual checks.

To print a sample check in a continuous-form printer

1. Insert the checks into your printer.

2. Select **W**-Write/Print Checks from the Main menu.

3. Press **Alt-P**-Print/Acct.

4. Select **P**-Print Checks, or press **Ctrl-P**.

5. Type in the Print Checks window the number of the printer you are using.

6. Type the number for the type of checks you are using.

7. Press **F9** to print the sample check. Do not move the check that is in your printer.

8. Look at the POINTER LINE that was just printed on the check. If your check did not print correctly, enter the position number to which the arrow is pointing at the prompt on the screen and press **Enter**. Repeat this step as necessary until the sample is printed correctly.

9. Press **Enter** when the checks are printed correctly.

10. Write down the correct position of the check for future reference.

To print a sample check in a laser printer

1. Make sure that Quicken is set to work with a laser printer. See *Printer Settings* for instructions.

2. Separate Quicken's sample continuous-form checks into groups of three and remove the tractor strips.

3. Insert the checks faceup into your laser printer paper tray with the top of the checks facing into the printer.

4. Select **W**-Write/Print Checks from the Main menu.

5. Press **Alt-P**-Print/Print.

6. Select **P**-Print Checks, or press **Ctrl-P**.

7. Type the number of the printer you are using and the number of the type of check you are using and press **Enter**.

8. Select **F9** to print a sample check. Do not move the checks in the printer.

9. Look at the POINTER LINE that was printed on your check. If the check did not print correctly, enter the position number to which the arrow is pointing at the prompt on the screen and press **Enter**. Repeat this step until the sample is printed correctly.

10. Press **Enter** when the checks are printed correctly.

11. Write down the correct position of the check for future reference.

Notes

Checks come in one of two different formats: continuous-form paper checks that work with traditional printers and printed pages of checks that work with a laser printer.

See also *Ordering Supplies* and *Printing Checks*.

═ **Postdating Checks** ═════════

Purpose

Dates checks in advance of when you write them.

To set a reminder about postdated checks

1. Select P-Set Preferences from the Main menu.

2. Select R-Automatic Reminder Settings.

3. Enter the number of days in which you want to be reminded of checks to be printed. Quicken can remind you from one to thirty days before the actual check date.

4. Press Enter or F10 to save the reminder setting.

To write postdated checks

1. Select A-Select Account from the Main menu.

2. Use the arrow keys to highlight your checking account. Press Enter.

3. You are in the Check Register screen. Press Ctrl-W to move to the Write Checks screen.

4. Change the current date in the Date blank to the date you want to appear on the check.

5. Enter the payee, dollar amount, optional comment, and category.

6. Press Enter or F10 to record the check.

To print postdated checks

1. Make sure that your checks are printing correctly. See *Positioning Checks in Your Printer* for instructions.

2. Select W-Write/Print checks from the Main menu.

3. Press Alt-P-Print/Acct.

4. Select P-Print Checks, or press Ctrl-P.

5. Fill in the number of the printer you are using.

6. Press A at the Print All/Selected Checks blank to print all checks, or press S to print only selected checks.

7. Type the number for the type of check you are using and press Enter.

8. If you are using a laser printer, type the number of additional copies (up to 3) you want, and indicate whether you are using a laser forms leader in your printer.

9. Press Enter.

10. If you chose to print selected checks, select the checks you want to print in the Select Checks to Print window and press Enter.

11. Enter the number of the next check you want to print in the Type Check Number window. Press Enter to begin printing checks.

12. Review the printed checks. Press Enter if all checks printed correctly. Otherwise, type the number of the first incorrectly printed check and press Enter to reprint.

13. Repeat step 12 until the checks print correctly.

Notes

Postdated checks appear in the Register with the date highlighted and are separated from other transactions by a double line.

Your current balance shows the balance in your account before any postdated transactions. Your ending balance shows the balance after all postdated transactions.

See also *Positioning Checks in Your Printer*.

Previewing Reports

Purpose

Enables you to view a report on the screen before printing a copy on paper.

Keys to use when previewing a report

Key(s)	Action
←	Scrolls left one column
→	Scrolls right one column
↓	Scrolls down one line
↑	Scrolls up one line
Tab	Moves right one column

Key(s)	Action
Shift-Tab	Moves left one column
Ctrl-←	Moves left one screen
Ctrl-→	Moves right one screen
PgUp	Moves up one screen
PgDn	Moves down one screen
Home	Moves to the far left of the current line
End	Moves to the far right of the current line
F1	Displays Help information
Ctrl-P	Prints report
F9	Switches to full column width. Works on only certain reports.

To display full descriptions in your report

1. Select C-Create Reports from the Main menu to select the report you want to use.

2. Enter the report information.

3. Generate the report. The report is displayed on the screen.

4. Press F9-Full Column Width to see the full descriptions for memo lines.

Print Report

Purpose

Enables you to select where you want to send the output. The Print Report window appears before you send anything to your printer.

To select your report output from the Print Report window

1. With a report displayed on-screen, press Ctrl-P to display the Print Report window.

2. Specify to which printer you want to send the output.

The first three choices refer to the printer output devices. These choices are the following:

1-Report Printer
2-Alt Report Printer
3-Check Printer

The other two options enable you to send the output to a file. These options are the following:

4-Disk (ASCII file)
5-Disk (1-2-3 file)

3. Press F9-Setup Printer to review the printer settings. Press Esc to return to the Print Report window.

4. Make sure that the paper is loaded correctly into your printer and that your printer is turned on and on-line.

5. Make sure that the Print To blank setting shows the printer you plan to use. Press Enter or F10.

Your output is processed, and the screen you were on before you started printing appears.

Note

See also *Printer Settings*.

Printer Settings

Purpose

Sets printer options for up to three different printers.

To assign printer settings

1. Select P-Set Preferences at the Main menu.

2. Select P-Printer Settings.

3. Select the printer for which you want to make changes.

4. Select either C-Settings for Printing Checks, R-Settings for Printing Reports, or A-Alternate Settings for Reports.

5. From the Printer List, use the arrow keys to highlight the type of printer you are using. Press Enter.

6. At the Style window, use the arrow keys to highlight the style of print you want to use. Press Enter.

7. The Printer Settings window is displayed next. Quicken automatically enters the printer settings based on the printer you selected from the Printer List. Make any necessary changes to the Printer Settings window.

8. Press F8-Edit Control Codes if you want to edit the printer control codes Quicken sends to your printer when it starts and stops printing. Consult your printer manual for your printer's codes.

9. Press F9-Select Printer From List if you want to reselect the printer you want to use.

10. Press Enter or F10 to set up the printer settings.

11. Repeat this procedure to set up the other two printer settings.

Notes

You can create three types of printer setups: the check printer, the report printer, and the alternate report printer.

If you have only one printer, you can set it up to work in several different ways.

Printing Checks

Purpose

Generates checks using Quicken and your computer's printer.

To find out how many checks need to be printed

1. Select W-Write/Print Checks from the Main menu.

2. Press Ctrl-P. Quicken shows the number of checks that need to be printed.

To print pending checks

1. Make sure that your checks are positioned correctly in your printer and that your printer is on-line.

2. Select **W**-Write/Print Checks from the Main menu.

3. Press **Alt-P**-Print/Acct.

4. Select **P**-Print Checks, or press **Ctrl-P**.

5. Enter the number of the printer you want to use and press **Enter**.

6. Press **A** at the Print All/Selected Checks blank if you want to print all checks. Press **S** if you want to print selected checks.

7. Enter the number for the type of check you are using and press **Enter**.

8. If you are using a laser printer, type the number of additional copies (up to 3) you want to print, and indicate whether you are using a laser forms leader in your printer. Press **Enter**.

9. Use the arrow keys to highlight the checks you want to print if you are printing only selected checks. Use the **space bar** to select those checks, or press **F9** to select all checks. Press **Enter** when you finish selecting checks.

10. Enter the number of the next check you want to print in the Type Check Number window. Press **Enter** to begin printing checks.

11. Press **Enter** at the Did Check Number Print Correctly window if the checks printed correctly. Otherwise, type the number of the first check that was printed incorrectly and press **Enter**.

12. Repeat step 11 until the checks print correctly.

Note

See also *Ordering Supplies* and *Positioning Checks in Your Printer*.

Printing Reports

Purpose

Generates and prints copies of your reports.

To generate a report

1. Select **C**-Create Reports from the Main menu, or press **Alt**-**R**-Reports from the Register or the Write Checks screen.

2. Select the type of report you want to create. You can select either:

   P-Personal Reports
   B-Business Reports
   I-Investment Reports
   M-Memorized Reports

   Or, you can select one of the following custom reports:

   T-Transaction
   S-Summary
   U-Budget
   A-Account Balances

3. Fill in the Create Report window and press **Enter** or **F10** to display the report on-screen.

For detailed printing information, refer to the individual report you want to generate.

To generate a custom report

1. Select **C**-Create Reports from the Main menu.

2. Select the type of report you want to create. You can select one of the following four reports:

   T-Transaction
   S-Summary
   U-Budget
   A-Account Balances

3. Type a report title in the first blank.

4. Enter the dates for which you want the information reported in the Restrict To Transactions From and Through blanks.

5. For Transaction reports, type the number that corresponds to the method for subtotalling the report. For Summary reports, type the number that

corresponds to the headings for rows and columns of the report. For Budget reports, type the number that corresponds to the column headings of the report. For Account Balances reports, type the number that corresponds to the intervals for balances to be reported.

6. Press **C** to base your report on the current account. Press **A** to base it on all accounts. Press **S** to base it on select accounts.

7. Select the accounts you want to use in your report if you chose to base your report on selected accounts. Use the arrow keys to highlight accounts. Press the **space bar** to toggle on or off the accounts.

8. Press **F8**-Options to set specific options.

9. Press **F9**-Filters to specify which transactions are included in the report.

10. Press **Esc** to return to the Create Report window, and then press **Ctrl-Enter** or **F10** to display the report on-screen.

11. Preview the report displayed on your screen; use the arrow keys to scroll the display.

12. Press **Ctrl-P**-Print when you are ready to print the report.

13. Enter the number of the printer you want to use if it is different from the default.

14. Press **Enter** or **F10** to print the report.

To generate a customized report

1. Select **C**-Create Reports from the Main menu.

2. Select **P**-Personal Reports or **B**-Business Reports.

3. Enter the type of report you want to generate.

   If you selected **P**-Personal Reports, you can select the following Personal reports:

   Cash Flow
   Itemized Categories
   Missing Check
   Monthly **B**udget

Net Worth
Tax Schedule
Tax Summary

If you selected **B**-Business Reports, you can select the following Business reports:

A/**P** by Vendor
A/**R** by Customer
Balance Sheet
Cash Flow
Job/Project
Missing Check
Pa**y**roll
P & L Statement

4. Enter an optional title and the dates you want the report to include.

5. Press **F8**-Options to display the Report Options window.

6. Fill in the Report Options window and press **Enter**.

7. Select the accounts you want to use in your report if the report is based on selected accounts. Use the arrow keys to highlight accounts. Press the **space bar** to toggle on and off accounts. Press **Ctrl-Enter** when you finish selecting reports.

8. Preview the report that is displayed on your screen; use the arrow keys to scroll the display.

9. Press **F9**-Filters to specify which transactions are included in the report.

10. Press **Esc** to return to the Create Report window, and then press **Ctrl-Enter** or **F10** to display the report on-screen.

11. Preview the report displayed on your screen; use the arrow keys to scroll the display.

12. Press **Ctrl-P**-Print when you are ready to print the report.

13. Enter the number of the printer you want to use if it is different from the default.

14. Press **Enter** or **F10** to print the report.

Notes

When you print a customized report, you determine the information your report includes. Setting a filter on your report enables you to define further the transactions your report includes.

See also *Filters*.

Pull-Down Menus

Purpose

Accesses Quicken's functions.

The functions of the pull-down menu items

Alt-H-Help

Provides context-sensitive Help.

Alt-P-Print/Acct

Selects, prints, backs up, exports, and imports information from other accounts.

Alt-E-Edit

Deletes, splits, finds, and moves different transactions.

Alt-S-Shortcuts

Memorizes transactions and enables you to recall memorized transactions and select categories, classes, and transaction groups.

Alt-R-Reports

Displays the menu of all available reports, including personal, business, and investment reports.

Alt-A-Activities

Reconciles your account, updates account balances, enables you to order supplies, accesses the pop-up calculator and loan calculator, and provides access to the operating system.

Quick Keys

Purpose

Enables you to assign your own Quick Key to accounts you use most often.

To assign a Quick Key to an account

1. Press **A**-Select Account from the Main menu.

2. Use the arrow keys to highlight the account to which you want to assign a Quick Key.

3. Press **Ctrl-E** to display the Edit Account Information window.

4. Press **Tab** to move to the Quick Key Assignment blank.

5. Type a number from **1–9**.

6. Press **Ctrl-Enter** to assign the Quick Key to the account.

To access an account using the Quick Key

From any screen, press **Ctrl** in combination with the Quick Key assigned to the account.

Note

Quicken displays the Quick Keys you assign to accounts in the Select Account To Use window. Quick Keys are shown in the first column to the right of the account name.

QuickZoom

Purpose

Enables you to examine the transaction detail behind a report entry.

To examine (QuickZoom) a report entry

1. Press **C**-Create Report from the Main menu.

2. Select the report you want to create from the next two menus.

3. With the report displayed on your screen, use the arrow keys to highlight the report entry you want to examine.

4. Press **Alt-F**-File.

5. Select **Z**-QuickZoom, or press **Ctrl-Z**.

6. Quicken displays a Transaction List window for Summary or Budget reports that lists all of the transactions that make up the report entry. For transaction reports, Quicken displays the Register entry that supports the report entry.

7. To display the Register entry for a transaction listed in the Transaction List window, use the arrow keys to highlight the transaction and press **F9**. Note that you cannot return to the Report screen from the Register screen.

8. Press **Esc** to remove the transaction detail from the screen.

Note

You can use the QuickZoom option only with Noninvestment Summary reports and Budget reports.

Reconciling Bank Accounts

Purpose

Verifies that your records in Quicken match those printed on your monthly bank statement.

To reconcile a bank account for the first time

1. Select **A**-Select Account from the Main menu.

2. Use the arrow keys to highlight your checking account. Press **Enter**.

3. Press **Alt-A**-Activities from the Register.

4. Select **E**-Reconcile from the Activities pull-down menu.

5. Enter the requested information in the Reconcile Register With Bank Statement window so that Quicken can process the reconciliation.

6. Compare the opening balance with the opening balance on your bank statement. If there is a difference, type the opening balance shown on your statement in the Reconcile Register With Bank Statement window and press **Enter**.

7. Type the ending balance shown on your bank statement and press **Enter**.

8. Enter any service charges that have been taken from your account as well as any interest you have received. Enter an appropriate category in which to place these adjustments. Quicken creates transactions in the register for these items.

9. Press **Ctrl-Enter** after you have filled in the Reconcile Register With Bank Statement window. Quicken then displays the uncleared transactions list and a Reconciliation Summary.

   Any difference between Quicken's opening balance and the bank's opening balance is shown in the Reconciliation Summary.

10. Mark transactions that are listed on your bank statement. To mark transactions as cleared, highlight them with the arrow keys and press **Enter**. Continue this procedure for all the checks appearing on your bank statement. Press the **space bar** to unmark a transaction.

11. Press **F8**-Mark Range to mark a range of checks. Enter the range of checks to mark as cleared and press **Enter**.

12. If you need to return to the Register to make any changes to transactions, press **F9** to display the Register. From the Register, press **F9** again to return to the uncleared transactions list.

13. Press **Ctrl-F10** when you finish marking your cleared transactions.

14. If there is a difference between Quicken's opening balance and the opening balance shown on your bank statement, Quicken will display the Create Opening Balance Adjustment window and ask if you want to record the difference as an adjustment to Quicken's opening balance. Press **Y** to record the adjustment, and then enter an optional category to which to assign the adjustment. Note that Quicken automatically records the adjustment in your Register.

If there is no difference between the Cleared
Transaction balance and the bank statement balance,
Quicken displays a congratulatory message and asks
if you want to print a Reconciliation Report.

15. If your bank account does not balance, mark
    transactions that have not yet been marked or
    unmark ones that have not gone through your
    account.

To reconcile a Quicken account after the first time

1. Select A-Select Account from the Main menu.

2. Use the arrow keys to highlight your checking
   account. Press Enter.

3. Press Alt-A-Activities from the Register.

4. Select E-Reconcile from the Activities pull-down
   menu.

5. Enter the requested information in the Reconcile
   Register With Bank Statement window so that
   Quicken can process the reconciliation.

6. Make sure that there is no difference between
   Quicken's opening balance and the opening balance
   shown on your statement. If there is a difference, see
   "To reconcile a bank account for the first time."

7. Type the ending balance shown on your bank
   statement and press Enter.

8. Enter any service charges that have been taken from
   your account as well as any interest you have
   received. Enter an appropriate category in which to
   place these adjustments. Quicken creates transactions
   in the register for these items.

9. Press Ctrl-Enter after you have filled in the
   Reconcile Register With Bank Statement window.
   Quicken then displays the uncleared transactions list
   and a Reconciliation Summary.

10. Mark transactions that are listed on your bank
    statement. To mark transactions as cleared, highlight
    them with the arrow keys and press Enter. Continue
    this for all the checks appearing on your bank
    statement. Press the space bar to unmark a
    transaction.

11. Press **F8**-Mark Range to mark a range of checks. Enter the range of checks to mark as cleared and press **Enter**.

12. If you need to return to the Register to make any changes to transactions, press **F9** to display the Register. From the Register, press **F9** again to return to the uncleared transactions list.

13. Press **Ctrl-F10** when you finish marking your cleared transactions.

14. If there is a difference between Quicken's opening balance and the opening balance shown on your bank statement, Quicken will display the Create Opening Balance Adjustment window and ask if you want to record the difference as an adjustment to Quicken's opening balance. Press **Y** to record the adjustment and then enter an optional category to assign the adjustment to. Note that Quicken automatically records the adjustment in your Register.

    If there is no difference between the Cleared Transaction balance and the bank statement balance, Quicken displays a congratulatory message and asks if you want to print a Reconciliation Report.

15. If your bank account does not balance, mark transactions that have not yet been marked or unmark ones that have not gone through your account.

16. Continue this procedure until the two balances are equal.

To add a balance adjustment entry in the Register

1. From the uncleared transactions list, press **Ctrl-F10** to reconcile your account.

2. Quicken displays the Adding Balance Adjustment Entry window and tells you the amount of the adjusting entry needed to balance your account.

3. Press **Y** to add the adjustment to the Register and press **Enter**.

4. Type an optional category name for the adjusting transaction.

5. Press **Enter** or **F10** to record the adjustment in the Register.

To print a reconciliation report

1. From the congratulatory message screen displayed after your bank account balances, press **Y** and press **Enter**.

2. Type the number of the printer to which you want to print the report and press **Enter**.

3. Type a different reconcile date if you want the date on the report to be different from today's date. Press **Enter**.

4. If you want a detailed report, change the **S** to **F** and press **Enter**.

5. Type a report title.

6. Press **Ctrl-Enter** or **F10** to begin printing.

Register

Purpose

Records transactions in your accounts.

To access the Register

Select **R**-Use Register from the Main menu, or press **Ctrl-R** from the Write Checks screen.

To create a new entry in the Register

1. Select **A**-Select Account from the Main menu.

2. Use the arrow keys to highlight the account whose Register you want to access. Press **Enter**.

3. Press **End** to move to the last blank in the Register.

4. Enter the information about the transaction. Press **Enter** or **Tab** after each entry to move to the next blank.

5. Type the date in the Date blank.

6. Enter the check number in the Num blank if you are working with a handwritten check. Use **+** and **–** to increase or decrease the check number by one. If you are not using handwritten checks, leave this blank empty. This blank is optional and not used in all types of accounts.

7. Type a word to identify the transaction in the Payee blank. If you are entering a transaction in your checking account Register, you should type the payee's exact name.

8. Enter the transaction amount in the Payment blank if it is a subtraction to your account.

9. Disregard the C column. The C (for Cleared) column is used to reconcile your account.

10. Enter the transaction amount in the Deposit blank if it is a deposit or an addition to your account.

   You should have an entry in either the Payment or Deposit blank, not both.

11. Add a transaction description in the Memo blank. (This step is optional.)

12. Type the name of the category and/or class in the Category blank to assign the transaction to a category or class that assists in creating custom reports. To select from a list of categories, press **Ctrl-C**.

13. Press **Enter** twice or **F10** to record the transaction.

To review entries in the Register

1. Select **A**-Select Account from the Main menu.

2. Use the arrow keys to highlight the account whose Register you want to review. Press **Enter**.

3. Use the arrow keys to highlight transactions in the Register.

4. Use **PgUp** or **PgDn** to move up or down one screen at a time.

5. Press **Ctrl-PgUp** to move to the beginning of the first entry in the month. Press **Ctrl-PgDn** to move to the first entry in the next month.

6. Press **Ctrl-Home** to see the first entry in the register.

7. Press **Ctrl-End** to see the last entry in the register.

To delete entries in the Register

1. Select **R**-Use Register from the Main menu.

2. Use the arrow keys to highlight the transaction you want to delete.

3. Press Alt-E-Edit.

4. Select D-Delete Transaction, or press Ctrl-D.

   The OK to Delete Transaction? window appears.

5. Select 1-Delete Transaction.

To use a different account Register

1. Press Ctrl-A to change accounts at any time while in the Register.

2. Use the arrow keys to highlight the account you want to use. Press Enter.

   Quicken displays the Register for the account you selected.

To print the Register

1. Select A-Select Account from the Main menu.

2. Use the arrow keys to highlight the account for which you want to print the register. Press Enter.

3. Press Alt-P-Print/Acct from the Register.

4. Select P-Print Register, or press Ctrl-P.

5. Fill in the blanks on the Print Register window to specify the transactions you want printed.

   Some blanks have default values entered. You can change these values or accept the defaults.

6. Specify the range of transactions you want to print in the Print Transactions From: MM/DD/YY To: MM/DD/YY blank.

7. Select the printer you want to use in the Print To blank.

8. Enter a title. If you don't enter a title, Quicken automatically titles the report "Register."

9. Press Y at the Print One Transaction Per Line blank if you want more transactions printed on each page. If you press N, Quicken prints each entry on three lines.

10. Press **Y** at the Print Transaction Splits blank to print the contents of split transactions.

11. Press **Y** at the Sort By Check Number blank to print the register to be sorted first by check number and then by date.

    Quicken defaults to sorting by date and then by check number.

12. Press **Enter** or **F10** to start printing the Register.

Report Layout

Purpose

Enables you to change the layout of reports as they are displayed on-screen.

To access the Layout menu from Report screens

1. Select **C**-Create Reports from the Main menu.

2. Select the report you want to create from the next two menus.

3. Quicken displays the report on your screen and a menu bar at the top of the screen.

4. Press **Alt**-**L**-Layout to display the Layout pull-down menu.

Layout options available from the Layout pull-down menu

E-**Hide/Show Cents** option lets you change the display of amounts in reports.

P-**Hide/Show Split** option enables you to change the display of split transactions in noninvestment transaction reports.

T-**Hide/Show Transactions** option enables you to change the display of transaction detail in transaction reports.

O-**Other Options** lets you access the Report Options window to set report options that vary by report type.

S-**Sort Transactions** option enables you to change the order of transactions in transaction reports.

R-**Row Headings** option lets you group and subtotal the transactions along the left side by various time intervals and criteria for Transaction and Summary reports.

H-**Column Headings** option lets you choose column headings for Summary, Budget, and Account Balances reports.

W-**Full Column Width** option lets you reduce or enlarge columns to half or full width in Transaction reports.

X-**Expand** option lets you display detail for report entries that have been summarized (collapsed) in Noninvestment Summary, Budget, and Account Balances Reports.

C-**Collapse** option lets you summarize report detail in Noninvestment Summary, Budget, and Account Balances reports.

Note

See also *Expand Reports, Collapse Reports,* and *Printing Reports.*

Report Options

Purpose

Enables you to specify how your reports are organized, the report format, and what type of transfers the reports include.

To access the Report Options window

Press **F8**-Options from any Report or Create Report window.

Report options available

Report options vary dependent upon the type of report you are generating. The following is a list of all report options:

Report organization

Select either **1**-Income And Expenses or **2**-Cash Flow Basis to specify how your report is organized. The

default setting is 1. For Account Balances reports, select
1-Net Worth Format or 2-Balance Sheet. The default
setting is 1.

Transfers

Press 3 to include only transfers to accounts outside the
report. Press 2 to exclude all types of transfers. Quicken
is generally set to include all transfers in the report (1).

Include unrealized gains

Press Y to include unrealized gains or losses from
investment accounts in your report. Press N to not
include them.

Memo/Category display

Select 1-Memo only to display only the memo from a
transaction, 2-Category only to display only the category
name, or 3-Display both (default) to display both the
memo and category name.

Show cents when displaying amounts

Press Y to show amounts with cents or N to show
amounts rounded to the nearest dollar.

Show totals only

Press Y to show only the dollar amount of transactions
in your report, or press N to list all the specified
transactions in your report.

Show split transaction detail

Press Y to show the detail included in the Split
Transaction window. Otherwise, press N.

Normal/Suppressed/Reversed subcategory display

Press N to display subcategories and subclasses in your
report. Press S to suppress the display of subcategories
and subclasses, or press R to group reports by
subcategory or subclasses with the corresponding
categories and classes grouped under them.

Note

Different reports offer different report options.

Restore File

Purpose

Restores your backed up data into Quicken format.

Note

See also *File Activities*.

Screen Colors

Purpose

Enables you to select from eight available screen color schemes.

To change to a monochrome screen setting

1. Select P-Set Preferences from the Main menu.

2. Select S-Screen Settings.

3. Select C-Screen Colors.

   A menu of available screen colors appears.

4. Select 1-Monochrome.

To use a color monitor

1. Select P-Set Preferences from the Main menu.

2. Select S-Screen Settings.

3. Select C-Screen Colors.

   A menu of available screen colors appears.

4. Select the color system you want to use. Quicken gives you the following choices:

   2-Reverse Monochrome
   3-Navy/Azure
   4-White/Navy
   5-Red/Gray
   6-Shades of Gray
   7-Purple/White
   8-Green/Yellow

To set screen colors if you are color-blind

1. Select **P**-Set Preferences from the Main menu.

2. Select **S**-Screen Settings.

3. Select **C**-Screen Colors.

   A menu of available screen colors appears.

4. Select **5**-Red/Gray.

   This setting is good for color-blind users of color monitors.

To display colors in shades of gray

1. Select **P**-Set Preferences from the Main menu.

2. Select **S**-Screen Settings.

3. Select **C**-Screen Colors.

   A menu of available screen colors appears.

4. Select **6**-Shades of Gray.

   This setting is good for one-color monitors such as those used on laptop computers.

Note

See also *Monitor Display*.

Selecting Accounts

Purpose

Enables you to choose the Quicken account you want to use.

To select an account

1. Select **A**-Select Account from the Main menu, or press **Ctrl-A** from within Quicken.

2. Use the arrow keys to highlight the account you want to use. Press **Enter**.

   The Register for the account you selected appears.

Notes

You can create, delete, or edit a Quicken account from the Select Account To Use window.

See also *Accounts*.

Select/Set Up File

Purpose

Creates or selects a Quicken file.

To select a file

1. Select P-Set Preferences from the Main menu.

2. Select F-File Activities.

3. Select S-Select/Set Up File.

4. Use the arrow keys to highlight the name of the Quicken file you want to access. Press Enter.

   The Select Account To Use window appears.

5. Select the account you want to use.

To set up a new account group

1. Select P-Set Preferences from the Main menu.

2. Select F-File Activities.

3. Select S-Select/Set Up File.

4. Use the arrow keys to highlight <Set Up File>. Press Enter.

5. Enter a DOS file name (up to eight characters) in the Set Up File window. Press Enter.

6. Specify the location of the new file. Enter a drive and pathname. Press Enter.

7. Indicate what standard categories you want to use.

   Press 1 to use the predefined home categories.
   Press 2 to use the business categories.
   Press 3 to use both home and business categories.
   Press 4 to use none of the standard categories.

8. Press **Enter**.

Quicken creates a new account group with the specified name.

Note

Accounts you set up are stored in the same file. There is no limit to the number of files you can set up. Unless you use Quicken for many different bookkeeping jobs, you probably need only one file. Each file is limited to 255 accounts.

Set File Location

Purpose

Specifies on which drive and directory a Quicken file is located.

To set the file location

1. Select **P**-Set Preferences from the Main menu.

2. Select **F**-File Activities.

3. Select **L**-Set File Location.

4. Type the name of a new directory or drive. Press **Enter**.

Note

Quicken looks for data files on only one disk drive or directory of your hard drive at a time. If you rename the subdirectory where Quicken is located, you need to set a new account group location.

Shell To DOS

Purpose

Enables you to exit Quicken temporarily so that you can use the operating system to format a disk or display a directory.

To exit to DOS

1. Select W-Write/Print Checks or R-Use Register from the Main menu.

2. Press Alt-A-Activities.

3. Select D-Use DOS.

   The system takes you to the DOS level.

4. Perform any operations you want in the operating system.

5. Type EXIT and press Enter to return to Quicken.

   Your data is intact, and you are returned to the place in Quicken from which you exited.

Note

You must have a minimum of 512K of RAM memory to use this feature.

Splitting Transactions

Purpose

Assigns more than one category to a transaction.

To split a transaction using amounts

1. Select W-Write/Print Checks or R-Use Register from the Main menu.

2. Use ↑ and ↓ to highlight the transaction to which you want to assign two or more categories.

3. Press Alt-E-Edit.

4. Select S-Split Transaction, or press Ctrl-S.

5. Quicken displays the Split Transaction window. Type the name of the first category or class for this transaction, or press Ctrl-C to choose the name from a list of names and press Enter.

6. Enter a description and press Enter. (This step is optional.)

7. Type the amount you want to apply to the first category.

8. Press Enter.

9. Continue to add categories you want to assign to the transaction.

10. Press Ctrl-Enter when you finish.

The Split Transaction window disappears and the Category blank contains the word SPLIT.

To split a transaction using percentages

1. Select W-Write/Print Checks or R-Use Register from the Main menu.

2. Use ↑ and ↓ to highlight the transaction to which you want to assign two or more categories.

3. Press Alt-E-Edit.

4. Select S-Split Transaction, or press Ctrl-S.

5. Quicken displays the Split Transaction window. Type the name of the first category or class for this transaction, or press Ctrl-C to choose the name from a list of names and press Enter.

6. Enter a description and press Enter. (This step is optional.)

7. Type the percentage of the transaction amount you want to apply to the first category. Percentages are entered as 00%.

8. Press Enter. Quicken enters the result in the Split Transaction window.

9. Continue to add categories and percentages you want to assign to the transaction.

10. Press Ctrl-Enter when you finish.

The Split Transaction window disappears and the Category blank contains the word SPLIT.

To copy information from one line to another

1. Type the first category or class for the transaction when the Split Transaction window appears, or press Ctrl-C to choose the category or class from a list.

2. Enter a description and press Enter. (This step is optional.)

3. Type the amount you want to apply to the first category and press Enter.

4. Type the quote mark (") as the first character in the second line if you want to repeat the category from the first line.

5. Continue entering split transactions.

To edit a split transaction

1. Select W-Write/Print Checks or R-Use Register from the Main menu.

2. Use the arrow keys to highlight the transaction you want to edit.

3. Press Alt-E-Edit.

4. Select S-Split Transaction, or press Ctrl-S.

5. Make any necessary changes to the Split Transaction window.

6. Press Ctrl-Enter when you finish making changes.

   Quicken saves the split and updates your transaction.

7. Press Enter-Enter or F10 to record the entire transaction.

To delete a line in a split transaction

1. Select W-Write/Print Checks or R-Use Register from the Main menu.

2. Use the arrow keys to highlight the transaction you want to edit.

3. Press Alt-E-Edit.

4. Select S-Split Transaction, or press Ctrl-S.

5. Use the arrow keys to highlight the line you want to delete.

6. Press Ctrl-D to delete the line from the Split Transaction window.

7. When you finish, press Ctrl-Enter.

8. Press Enter-Enter or F10 to record the transaction.

To delete a split transaction

1. Select **W**-Write/Print Checks or **R**-Use Register from the Main menu.

2. Use the arrow keys to highlight the transaction you want to edit.

3. Press **Alt-E**-Edit.

4. Select **S**-Split Transaction, or press **Ctrl-S**.

5. Highlight each line and press **Ctrl-D** to delete each line from the Split Transaction window.

6. When you finish, press **Ctrl-Enter**.

   The word SPLIT disappears from the Category column.

7. Press **Enter-Enter** or **F10** to record the entire transaction.

To use split transactions for a long memo field

1. Select **W**-Write/Print Checks or **R**-Use Register from the Main menu.

2. Highlight the transaction for which you want to create a long memo.

3. Press **Alt-E**-Edit.

4. Select **S**-Split Transaction, or press **Ctrl-S**.

5. Type the extended memo in the Description column. When you reach the end of a line, press **Enter** three times to move to the next line.

6. Press **Ctrl-Enter** when you finish.

Notes

If you use voucher checks, Quicken prints the first fifteen lines of information from the Split Transaction window on the voucher.

You also can use the Split Transaction window as a note pad to clarify a transaction's purpose. These comments print on the first fifteen lines of your voucher check.

Start New Year

Purpose

Archives prior year transactions and clears the current file.

Note

See *Year End File Activities*.

Starting Quicken

Purpose

Begins executing the program.

To start Quicken

1. Begin at the DOS prompt. Change to the directory where you installed Quicken.

   If you used the default settings when installing the program, type **CD\QUICKEN5**.

2. Press **Enter**.

3. Press **Q**.

4. Press **Enter**.

   DOS loads Quicken, and the Main menu appears.

Subcategories

Purpose

Specifies how your income and expenses are used.

To create a new subcategory

1. Select **W**-Write/Print Checks or **R**-Use Register from the Main menu.

2. Press **Alt-S**-Shortcuts.

3. Select **C**-Categorize/Transfer, or press **Ctrl-C**.

   The Category and Transfer List appears, which lists both categories and subcategories.

4. Press **Home** to highlight `<New Category>`. Press **Enter**.

   The Set Up Category window appears.

5. Type the name of the subcategory after the prompt.

6. Press **S** to specify that it is a subcategory.

7. Type a description. (This step is optional.)

8. Press **Y** if the subcategory is tax-related. Press **N** if it is not.

9. Press **F9** to assign a tax schedule to this subcategory.

10. Use ↑ and ↓ to select the tax schedule for this subcategory. Press **Enter**.

11. Use ↑ and ↓ to select the tax line for this subcategory. Press **Enter**.

12. Press **F10** to add the new subcategory to the Category and Transfer List.

To assign a subcategory to a transaction

1. Select **W**-Write/Print Checks or **R**-Use Register from the Main menu.

2. Enter transaction information in the Write Checks screen or the Register.

3. Type the category name followed by a :. Then type the subcategory name. Or, press **Ctrl-C** to display the Category and Transfer List. Use the arrow keys to select a subcategory from the list and press **Enter**.

4. Press **Enter-Enter** or **F10** to record the transaction.

To delete a subcategory

1. Select **W**-Write/Print Checks or **R**-Use Register from the Main menu.

2. Press **Alt-S**-Shortcuts.

3. Select **C**-Categorize/Transfer, or press **Ctrl-C**.

   The Category List appears, which lists both categories and subcategories.

4. Use the arrow keys to highlight the subcategory you want to delete.

5. Press **Ctrl-D**.

6. Type **YES** to confirm the deletion.

7. Press **Enter**.

   The subcategory is deleted and removed from memory.

To edit a subcategory

1. Select **W**-Write/Print Checks or **R**-Use Register from the Main menu.

2. Press **Alt-S**-Shortcuts.

3. Select **C**-Categorize/Transfer, or press **Ctrl-C**.

   The Category List appears, which lists both categories and subcategories.

4. Use the arrow keys to highlight the subcategory you want to edit.

5. Press **Ctrl-E**.

   Quicken displays the Edit Category window.

6. Enter a new subcategory name at the Name blank.

7. Change the description. A description is not required, but it is helpful.

8. Press **Y** or **N** to tell Quicken if the category is tax related.

9. Press **F9** to assign or make changes to the tax schedule for the subcategory.

10. When you finish making changes, press **Ctrl-Enter** from any blank in the window.

    Quicken makes the changes to all previous transactions assigned to this subcategory in the Register.

To promote a subcategory to a category

1. Select **W**-Write/Print Checks or **R**-Use Register from the Main menu.

2. Press **Alt-S**-Shortcuts.

3. Select **C**-Categorize/Transfer, or press **Ctrl-C**.

   The Category List appears, which lists both categories and subcategories.

4. Use the arrow keys to highlight the subcategory you want to change to a category.

5. Press **F8**.

6. Press **Home** to move the subcategory to the top of the Category and Transfer List.

7. Press **Enter**. Quicken changes the subcategory to a category and positions the name alphabetically in the Category and Transfer List.

   Quicken makes the changes to all previous transactions assigned to this subcategory in the Register.

To move a subcategory to another category

1. Select **W**-Write/Print Checks or **R**-Use Register from the Main menu.

2. Press **Alt-S**-Shortcuts.

3. Select **C**-Categorize/Transfer, or press **Ctrl-C**.

   The Category List appears, which lists both categories and subcategories.

4. Use the arrow keys to highlight the subcategory you want to move to another category.

5. Press **F8**. Quicken moves the subcategory to the same line as its parent category. A + (plus) sign at the end of the subcategory name indicates that the subcategory contains subcategories. These subcategories will also be moved to another category.

6. Use the arrow keys to move the subcategory to the new category for which you want it to be a subcategory.

7. Press **Enter**. Quicken moves the subcategory under the new category.

   Quicken makes the changes to all previous transactions assigned to the subcategory in the Register.

Subclasses

Purpose

Works with classes to group and subtotal similar classes together.

To create a new subclass

1. Press Alt-S-Shortcuts from the Write Checks screen or the Register.

2. Select L-Select/Set Up Class, or press Ctrl-L.

   The Class List window appears, which lists the classes and subclasses currently defined for the account.

3. Press Home to highlight <New Class> and press Enter.

4. Enter the name (up to 15 characters) of the subclass in the Name blank in the Set Up Class window.

5. Type a description of the subclass after the Description blank. (This step is optional.)

6. Press Enter. Quicken adds the new subclass to your list.

To assign a subclass to a transaction

1. Select W-Write/Print Checks or R-Use Register from the Main menu.

2. Enter transaction information in the Write Checks screen or the Register.

3. In the Category field, type the category name followed by a /. Then type the class name followed by a :. Type the subclass name after the colon. Or, press Ctrl-L to display the Class List. Use the arrow keys to select a subclass from the list and press Enter.

4. Press Enter-Enter or F10 to record the transaction.

To delete a subclass

1. Press **Alt-S**-Shortcuts from the Write Checks screen or the Register.

2. Select **L**-Select/Set Up Class, or press **Ctrl-L**.

   The Class List window appears, which lists the classes and subclasses currently defined.

3. Use the arrow keys to highlight the subclass you want to delete.

4. Press **Ctrl-D**.

   Quicken prompts you to make sure that you want to delete the subclass.

5. Press **Enter** to delete the subclass. Press **Esc** to abort the deletion.

To edit a subclass

1. Press **Alt-S**-Shortcuts from the Write Checks screen or the Register.

2. Select **L**-Select/Set Up Class, or press **Ctrl-L**.

   The Class List window appears, which lists the classes and subclasses currently defined.

3. Use the arrow keys to highlight the subclass you want to edit.

4. Press **Ctrl-E**.

5. Enter a new name and/or description for the subclass in the Edit Class window.

   All the transactions in your Quicken file that reference this subclass receive the changes you make.

6. Press **Enter** to save the changes.

To print a list of classes and subclasses

1. Press **Alt-S**-Shortcuts from the Write Checks screen or the Register.

2. Select **L**-Select/Set Up Class, or press **Ctrl-L**.

   The Class List window appears, which lists all the classes and subclasses that are currently defined.

3. Press **Ctrl-P** to print the entire list.

4. Select the printer you want to use if it is different from the default.

5. Press **Enter** or **F10** to print the list.

Notes

Subclasses enable you to specify a transaction's payee, location, and date. Quicken does not come with a standard set of subclasses.

You must list classes and categories correctly in a multiple class entry. Always type the more general class first, followed by a more specific class. This organization ensures that the class is the primary class in related reports.

Tax Schedules

Purpose

Allocates transactions to a specific tax schedule and line within the tax schedule.

Notes

Tax schedules are assigned to categories/subcategories at the Set Up Category window.

See *Categories*.

Tax Schedule Personal Report

Purpose

Lists transactions assigned to categories with tax schedule information.

To generate a Tax Schedule report

1. Select **C**-Create Reports from the Main menu.

2. Select **P**-Personal Reports.

3. Select **S**-Tax Schedule.

4. Type a title for the report and press **Enter**. (This step is optional.)

5. Type the starting and ending dates for the report and press **Enter**.

6. Preview the report by using the arrow keys to scroll the display.

7. Press **Ctrl-P**-Print when you are ready to print the report.

8. Enter the number of the printer you are using if it is different from the default.

9. Press **Enter** or **F10** to print the report.

Notes

You can use the Tax Schedule report at the end of the calendar year to help prepare your income tax return.

See *Categories*.

Tax Summary Personal Report

Purpose

Displays all the transactions in your account register that are assigned to tax-related categories.

To generate a Tax Summary report

1. Select **C**-Create Reports from the Main menu.

2. Select **P**-Personal Reports.

3. Select **T**-Tax Summary.

4. Enter a title and the months between which you want to base the balances. Press **Enter**.

5. Preview the report that is displayed on your screen; use the arrow keys to scroll the display.

6. Press **Ctrl-P**-Print when you are ready to print.

7. Enter the number of the printer you want to use if it is different from the default.

8. Press **Enter** or **F10** to print the report.

Note

See also *Customize Report* and *Filters*.

Transaction Groups

Purpose

Groups recurring transactions you pay or add to your account at the same time.

To memorize a transaction for a transaction group

1. Select **W**-Write/Print Checks or **R**-Use Register from the Main menu.

2. Enter the transaction into the Write Checks screen or the Register.

3. Press **Alt-S**-Shortcuts.

4. Select **M**-Memorize Transaction, or press **Ctrl-M**.

   Quicken asks you to confirm that you want to memorize the information.

5. Press **Enter** to memorize the transaction.

   You are returned to the Write Checks screen or the Register.

6. Press **Enter-Enter** or **F10** to complete the transaction you entered. If you do not want to record the transaction in the Register or Write Checks screen, press **Ctrl-D** to delete it.

To create a transaction group

1. Select **W**-Write/Print Checks or **R**-Use Register from the Main menu.

2. Make sure that all the transactions you want to include in this transaction group have been memorized.

3. Press **Alt-S**-Shortcuts.

4. Select **G**-Transaction Groups, or press **Ctrl-J**.

5. Use the arrow keys to highlight the first <unused> transaction group. Press **Enter**.

   The Describe Group # window appears.

6. Type the name for this transaction group in the first blank and press **Enter**.

7. Enter the account to load before executing and press **Enter**.

   The Select Account window appears if your choice does not match existing accounts.

8. Press the number that corresponds to how often you want the group to be scheduled and press **Enter**.

   1 for no regular scheduling
   2 for weekly scheduling
   3 for scheduling every two weeks
   4 for scheduling twice a month
   5 for scheduling every four weeks
   6 for monthly scheduling
   7 for quarterly scheduling
   8 for biannual scheduling
   9 for annual scheduling

9. Enter the date when you first want to be reminded that the group is due.

10. Press **Ctrl-Enter** to record the information in the Describe Group # window.

    The Assign Transaction To Group window appears.

11. Use the arrow keys to highlight each transaction you want to include in this transaction group. Press the **space bar** to assign highlighted transactions to the new transaction group. Select as many transactions as you want your group to include.

12. Press **Enter**. Your transaction group is created.

To execute a transaction group

1. Select **W**-Write/Print Checks or **R**-Use Register from the Main menu.

2. Press **Alt-S**-Shortcuts.

3. Select **G**-Transaction Groups, or press **Ctrl-J**.

   The Transaction Group To Execute window appears.

4. Use the arrow keys to highlight the group you want to execute. Press **Enter**.

   If a date is scheduled for the group, it is displayed in the Transaction Group Date window. This is the date that Quicken gives the transactions when it enters them into your Register.

5. Change the date or accept the current date. Press **Enter**.

6. Quicken displays a message saying that the transactions from the group have been entered in the account Register. Press **Enter**.

7. Make any changes you want to the transactions in the Register.

8. Press **Enter-Enter** or **F10** when you finish making changes.

To add a transaction to a transaction group

1. Select **W**-Write/Print Checks or **R**-Use Register from the Main menu.

2. Make sure that the transaction you want to include in the transaction group has been memorized.

3. Press **Alt-S**-Shortcuts.

4. Select **G**-Transaction Groups, or press **Ctrl-J**.

5. Use the arrow keys to highlight the group to which you want to add transactions. Press **Ctrl-E**.

   The Describe Group # window appears with information about the group.

6. Press **Ctrl-Enter** to see the list of memorized transactions you can assign to a group.

   The Assign Transaction To Group window appears.

7. Assign a transaction to your new group by using the arrow keys to highlight the transaction you want to include. Press the **space bar** to assign the transaction to the transaction group. Select as many transactions as you want in your group.

8. Press **Enter** to add the transaction(s) to the transaction group.

To edit a transaction group

1. Select **W**-Write/Print Checks or **R**-Use Register from the Main menu.

2. Press **Alt-S**-Shortcuts.

3. Select **G**-Transaction Groups, or press **Ctrl-J**.

4. Use the arrow keys to highlight the group you want to edit. Press **Ctrl-E**.

5. Make any changes you want to the Describe Group # window. Press **Ctrl-Enter**.

   The Assign Transactions To Group window appears.

6. Use the arrow keys to highlight transactions. Press the **space bar** to either include or remove the transaction from the transaction group.

7. Press **Enter** to save the changes to the transaction group.

To delete a transaction group

1. Select **W**-Write/Print Checks or **R**-Use Register from the Main menu.

2. Press **Alt-S**-Shortcuts.

3. Select **G**-Transaction Groups, or press **Ctrl-J**.

4. Use the arrow keys to highlight the group you want to delete.

5. Press **Ctrl-D** to delete the transaction group.

Note

When you tell Quicken to pay a transaction group, it creates the necessary Register entries for you automatically. Quicken reminds you when it is time to pay the transactions in a group; Quicken will not execute or pay the transaction group automatically.

Transaction Settings

Purpose

Enables you to adjust transaction settings to fit your needs.

Explanations of transaction setting options

Beep when recording and memorizing(Y/N)

Press **N** to turn off the beep you hear when recording or memorizing a transaction.

Request confirmation when modifying a transaction(Y/N)

Press N to prevent Quicken from asking you to confirm every modification. Remember that if you take out this request confirmation, you need to be careful not to edit or type over information you did not intend to remove.

Request confirmation when deleting or voiding a transaction(Y/N)

Press N to prevent Quicken from asking you to confirm every deletion or void. Remember that if you take out this request confirmation, you need to be careful not to delete information you did not intend to remove.

Enter dates as MM/DD/YY or DD/MM/YY(M/D)

Press M to display the date in month/day/year format or D to display the date in day/month/year format.

Require a category on transactions(Y/N)

Press Y so that Quicken makes sure that you have specified a category every time you enter a transaction in the Register or the Write Checks screen. Setting this to Y ensures that the information in your reports is accurately categorized.

Show Memo/Category/Both in register(M/C/B)

Press either M, C, or B to determine what information is displayed on the second line of the Payee Memo Category column in the Register when the transaction is not highlighted.

Exact matches on finds and filters(Y/N)

Press Y for Quicken to find text only if it matches exactly the text you typed in the field. Press N for Quicken to find text if it appears anywhere in the field.

To change the transaction settings

1. Select P-Set Preference from the Main menu.

2. Select T-Transaction Settings.

3. Use Enter, Tab, and Shift-Tab to move the cursor through the blanks. Change the settings for the option(s).

4. Press Enter or F10 to save the transaction settings.

Transferring Money between Accounts

Purpose

Transfers money between accounts and automatically creates a Register entry for you.

To transfer money between accounts

1. Select **W**-Write/Print Checks or **R**-Use Register from the Main menu.

2. Fill out the transaction entry in the usual manner.

3. At the Category blank, press **Ctrl-C** to display the Category and Transfer List.

4. Use the arrow keys to highlight the name of the account to or from which you want to transfer money and press **Enter**. Note that accounts are listed at the end of the Category and Transfer List.

   You see the account name enclosed in brackets ([ ]) on the Register after the transfer is recorded.

5. Press **Enter-Enter** or **F10** to record the transaction.

   Quicken records the transaction in the current account Register and creates a duplicate transaction in the account Register for the account to or from which you transferred money.

To find a duplicate transfer transaction

1. Select **W**-Write/Print Checks or **R**-Use Register from the Main menu.

2. Highlight the transfer transaction.

3. Press **Alt-E**-Edit.

4. Select **T**-Go To Transfer, or press **Ctrl-X**.

   The entry for the transfer account appears. The transfer transaction is highlighted so that you can find it.

5. Press **Ctrl-X** to return to the previous transaction. Your original transaction appears.

Notes

When you write a check to pay your credit card bill, you enter a transaction into your checking account Register. At the same time, Quicken creates a corresponding entry in your credit card account Register with the correct deposit made to your credit card account.

Whenever you transfer funds, the account name to which you transfer is enclosed in brackets ([ ]). You see these bracketed accounts in the Category and Transfer List and in the Category blank of the transaction.

Tutorials and Assistants

Purpose

Provides an overview of Quicken and gives on-screen demonstration for first time set-up procedures.

To use tutorials and assistants

1. Select **T**-Use Tutorials/Assistants from the Main menu.

2. Select one of the following:

   S-First Time Set Up if you are a new Quicken user and need help getting started
   O-Quicken Overview if you want a brief presentation on the program features
   T-Set Up Quick Tour if you want to experiment with Quicken and enter the sample data from the Quicken User Manual
   F-Create New File if you need help setting up a Quicken file
   A-Create New Account if you want assistance in setting up an account
   P-Create Payroll Support if you want Quicken to set up payroll categories and accounts you can use in your small business

Update Account Balances

Purpose

Revises the balance in other asset, other liability, and cash accounts to accurately reflect the value in the accounts.

To update the balance in an Other Asset account

1. Select A-Select Account from the Main menu.

2. Use the arrow keys to select the other asset account you want to update. Press Enter.

3. From the account Register, press Alt-A-Activities.

4. Select U-Update Account Balances to display the Update Account Balance window.

5. Type the current value of the other asset account and press Enter.

6. Type a category name for the adjusting transaction and press Enter. (This step is optional.)

7. Change the adjustment date if necessary.

8. Press Ctrl-Enter to update the balance.

To update the balance in an Other Liability account

1. Select A-Select Account from the Main menu.

2. Use the arrow keys to select the other liability account you want to update. Press Enter.

3. From the account Register, press Alt-A-Activities.

4. Select U-Update Account Balances to display the Update Account Balance window.

5. Type the current value of the other liability account and press Enter.

6. Type a category name for the adjusting transaction and press Enter. (This step is optional.)

7. Change the adjustment date if necessary.

8. Press Ctrl-Enter to update the balance.

To update the balance in a Cash account

1. Select A-Select Account from the Main menu.

2. Use the arrow keys to select the cash account you want to update. Press Enter.

3. From the account Register, press Alt-A-Activities.

4. Select U-Update Account Balances to display the Update Account Balance window.

5. Type the current value of the cash account and press Enter.

6. Type a category name for the adjusting transaction and press Enter. (This step is optional.)

7. Change the adjustment date if necessary.

8. Press Ctrl-Enter to update the balance.

Notes

If the value of assets, liabilities, or cash you entered is more than the account balance, Quicken enters an adjustment in the Increase column of the Register. If the value of assets, liabilities, or cash is less than the account balance, Quicken enters an adjustment in the Decrease column of the Register.

To ensure that Net Worth and Account Balances reports are accurate, you should periodically update your account balances.

Update Prices

Purpose

Enables you to update the market price of securities in your investment accounts.

Note

See *Investment Accounts*.

Voiding Transactions

Purpose

Nullifies a transaction in the account Register without deleting a record of it.

To void a check

1. Select A-Select Account from the Main menu.

2. Use the arrow keys to highlight your checking account. Press Enter.

3. Use the arrow keys to highlight the check you want to mark void in the Check Register.

4. Press Alt-E-Edit.

5. Select V-Void Transaction, or press Ctrl-V.

    The check is marked as void.

Writing Checks

Purpose

Prints personalized checks using Quicken and your computer's printer.

To fill out a check

1. Press Alt-A from the Main menu to display the Select Account To Use window.

2. Use the arrow keys to highlight your checking account. Press Enter.

    The Check Register appears.

3. Press Alt-A-Activities.

4. Select W-Write Checks, or press Ctrl-W.

    If your checking account is already the current account, select W-Write/Print Checks from the Main menu to access the Write Checks screen.

5. Enter the date you want on the check when you print it. Use + and – to change the date. Or press:

    T   to change the date to today's date
    M   to change the date to the first day of the current month
    H   to change the date to the last day of the current month
    Y   to change the date to the first day of the current year
    R   to change the date to the last day of the current year

    Press Enter when the date is correct.

6. Type the name of the check's payee. Press Enter.

7. Type the amount of the check in the Dollars blank and press Enter.

    Quicken spells out the dollar amount for you on the next line.

8. Enter any information you want on the next five lines.

   If you are mailing the check in an envelope with a clear window on the front, enter the payee's name and address.

9. Type a message in the Memo blank to inform the payee of the check's purpose.

10. Type a category or class for this transaction in the Category blank, or press **Ctrl-C** or **Ctrl-L** to choose the category or class name from a list of names.

11. Press **Enter-Enter** or **F10** to record the check.

    The check is recorded in the Check Register.

To edit a check

1. Select **W**-Write/Print Checks from the Main menu to display the Write Checks screen.

   If you are in the Register, press **Alt-A**-Activities and then select **W**-Write Checks; or press **Ctrl-W**.

2. Use **PgUp** and **PgDn** to find the check you want to edit.

   Use **Ctrl-Home** to go to the first check or **Ctrl-End** to go to the last check.

3. Make any necessary changes to the check by typing over the entries in the Write Checks screen.

4. Press **Ctrl-Enter** to record the changes. Press **Esc** to cancel the changes.

To delete a check

1. Select **W**-Write/Print Checks from the Main menu to display the Write Checks screen.

   If you are in the Register, press **Alt-A**-Activities and then select **W**-Write Checks; or press **Ctrl-W**.

2. Use **PgUp** and **PgDn** to find the check you want to delete.

   Use **Ctrl-Home** to go to the first check or **Ctrl-End** to go to the last check.

3. Press **Alt-E**-Edit.

4. Select **D**-Delete Transaction, or press **Ctrl-D**.

   Quicken makes sure that you want to delete this check by displaying an OK To Delete Transaction? window.

5. Select **1**-Delete Transaction, or press **Enter** to confirm the deletion.

   The check is deleted from the screen and from the check Register.

Notes

The bottom of the Write Checks screen has valuable information about your account. The account you are using is displayed on the lower left side of the screen.

The right side of the screen displays several different balances.

   The Checks to Print balance displays the current total for checks you have written and not yet printed. The Current Balance appears if you have postdated checks, and it displays your balance as of the current date.
   The Ending Balance is calculated every time you record a check to tell you the new balance of your account.

Any time you write a check from your checking account at the Write Checks screen, Quicken automatically creates a corresponding entry in the Check Register.

Year End File Activities

Purpose

Closes a Quicken file at the end of an accounting period, with the Archive option or the Start New Year option.

To archive prior year transactions and keep the current file intact

1. Select **P**-Set Preferences from the Main menu.

2. Select **F**-File Activities.

3. Select Y-Year End to display the Year End window.

4. Press 1-Archive to display the Archive File window.

5. Make any necessary changes to the file name, archive file location, and the archive transaction dates.

6. Press Ctrl-Enter to create the archive file.

To archive prior year transactions and clear the current file

1. Select P-Set Preferences from the Main menu.

2. Select F-File Activities.

3. Select Y-Year End to display the Year End window.

4. Press 2-Start New Year to display the Start New Year window.

5. Type a name for the archive file that Quicken will create and press Enter.

6. Make any necessary changes to the start date or the location for the current file.

7. Press Ctrl-Enter to create the archive file and delete transactions from the prior year. Note that investment transactions and uncleared transactions are not deleted from the current file.

8. Specify whether you want to use the current file or the archive file.

Notes

The Archive option copies all transactions from the prior year to an archive file. Prior year transactions are *not* deleted from the current file.

The Start New Year option copies all transactions from the prior year to an archive file and then deletes the transactions from the current file. Investment transactions and uncleared transactions are never deleted.

Index